MAKING THE MOST OF YOUR
VETERANS AFFAIRS (VA) HOME LOAN BENEFITS

An Active Duty Service Member and Veteran's Guide to Home Ownership

By David E. Nelson, Jr.

MAKING THE MOST OF YOUR VETERANS AFFAIRS (VA) HOME LOAN BENEFITS AN ACTIVE DUTY SERVICE MEMBER AND VETERAN'S GUIDE TO HOME OWNERSHIP

1405 SW 6th Avenue • Ocala, Florida 34471 • Phone 800-814-1132 • Fax 352-622-1875
Website: www.atlantic-pub.com • Email: sales@atlantic-pub.com
SAN Number: 268-1250

Library of Congress Cataloging-in-Publication Data

Names: Nelson, David, 1975- author.
Title: Making the most of your Veterans Affairs (VA) home : an active duty service member and veteran's guide to home ownership loan benefits / by David Nelson.
Description: Ocala, Florida : Atlantic Publishing Group, Inc., [2017] | Includes bibliographical references and index.
Identifiers: LCCN 2017053851 (print) | LCCN 2017055743 (ebook) | ISBN 9781620235225 (ebook) | ISBN 9781620235218 (pbk. : alk. paper) | ISBN 1620235218 (alk. paper)
Subjects: LCSH: Veterans—Loans—United States. | House buying—United States. | Mortgage loans—Law and legislation—United States. | United States. Veterans Administration.
Classification: LCC UB357 (ebook) | LCC UB357 .N375 2017 (print) | DDC 362.86/82—dc23
LC record available at https://lccn.loc.gov/2017053851

Printed in the United States

PROJECT MANAGER: Danielle Lieneman
INTERIOR LAYOUT AND COVER DESIGN: Nicole Sturk

Reduce. Reuse.
RECYCLE.

A decade ago, Atlantic Publishing signed the Green Press Initiative. These guidelines promote environmentally friendly practices, such as using recycled stock and vegetable-based inks, avoiding waste, choosing energy-efficient resources, and promoting a no-pulping policy. We now use 100-percent recycled stock on all our books. The results: in one year, switching to post-consumer recycled stock saved 24 mature trees, 5,000 gallons of water, the equivalent of the total energy used for one home in a year, and the equivalent of the greenhouse gases from one car driven for a year.

Over the years, we have adopted a number of dogs from rescues and shelters. First there was Bear and after he passed, Ginger and Scout. Now, we have Kira, another rescue. They have brought immense joy and love not just into our lives, but into the lives of all who met them.

We want you to know a portion of the profits of this book will be donated in Bear, Ginger and Scout's memory to local animal shelters, parks, conservation organizations, and other individuals and nonprofit organizations in need of assistance.

*— **Douglas & Sherri Brown**,*
President & Vice-President of Atlantic Publishing

Table of Contents

Foreword

David Nelson has written the Bible for service members and veterans to use their VA home loan benefits. It's an amazing tool to have access to. I encourage everyone, whether you are active-duty military, a veteran, or even a civilian to read this book. While reading *Making the Most of Your VA Home Loan Benefits,* I realized that David had a truly unique advantage to have been on both sides of the table when it comes to purchasing homes as a service member and real estate agent. He didn't just write about the home buying journey, but he takes the reader through the process step-by-step, without missing a beat, from obtaining the loan to the final walk through and closing.

I am an associate broker and manager at 1st Class Real Estate in the Hampton Roads area of Virginia that have been assisting military families for nearly 10 years with the sale and purchasing of properties. As a certified military residential and relocation specialist, I spent the majority of my career working with service members and veterans. Due to my qualifications and outstanding reputation with in the Hampton Roads community, David approached me with the opportunity to review and contribute to his book with my honest unbiased professional opinion. Prior to publication I was ecstatic that we got a chance to meet to hear his story and ideas to remove the fear from service members and veterans about purchasing homes.

While still on active duty, David took it upon himself to attend night classes to obtain his real estate license simply just to learn about the process before actually purchasing his first home. That decision led David to an interesting career as a realtor. I found it to be both incredible and sad that he felt that he had to go to such lengths to get information to utilize a benefit that belongs to him, but many service members feel the same way as he did. Purchasing a home with the VA home loan benefits is one of the best financial advantages of serving. In this book David also went through great lengths to obtain quality resources for his readers to use, including a credit repair specialist, his personal loan officer, and numerous real estate agents (that he personally researched) around the country in many highly populated military cities that specialize in assisting veterans.

This book will help service members and veterans potentially build future wealth by purchasing income properties. Veterans now have a manual available to them from one of their brothers in uniform. It is obvious after reading this book that he is someone who has been through the home buying process multiple times as an active duty service member and a real estate professional. David has the blueprint in these pages, and now it is yours.

Cassandra Simpson
Associate Broker
Manager
CMRS, MRP, ABR, CSR
COE Award Winner
1st Class Real Estate
Hampton Roads Virginia
757-751-0482
Letsimpsonsellit@gmail.com

Introduction

There are plenty of books out there for first-time home buyers, but not too many for veterans explaining how to properly use their VA Home Loan to purchase properties. In the military we tend to be mainly focused on our training exercises or mission at hand and forget to take care of our future financial health. I'm not expressing how I feel, or what someone told me secondhand or what I saw on TV; I am writing about what I have been through firsthand. Furthermore, everything that I express to you in this book is from personal experience as a veteran, as a VA Home Loan recipient and as an Active real estate agent. No one taught me how to purchase properties using our VA Home Loan benefits when I was a young sailor, and that is why I feel as if it's my personal duty to share this information with you, from all perspectives, so that you know how to use the system to your utmost advantage.

There are currently approximately 18.8 million veterans in this country, but only 4 percent of us have actually used our VA Home Loan benefits. If you are a part of the 96 percent (18,040,000) of veterans that have not taken advantage of this benefit, ask yourself: why?

Here are some real life answers I've gotten when I ask my fellow veterans and active duty service members the same question — *Why haven't you taken advantage of your VA Home Loan benefits?* — along with my responses.

I've been out of the military too long.

My response: No you haven't, because the VA Home Loan benefits do not dissolve over time.

I have not been in the military long enough to purchase a home.

My response: Not true, if you have been in longer than six months on active duty.

I don't want to live in this area for the rest of my life so I will continue to rent. Or I am waiting to go to my next duty station.

My response: You can use your VA Home Loan benefits an unlimited number of times and you can relocate as many times as you desire.

I don't have any money to buy a home (while wearing a pair of $250 shoes, $175 watch, $300 shirt and pants combined and $500 worth of jewelry).

My response: First of all, your current complete outfit cost more money than what you might need to purchase a home using your VA Home Loan benefits. Furthermore, with help from the right realtor and loan officer you could possibly not have to bring any money with you to closing.

I already used my VA Home Loan and need to sell my house first.

My response: No, you can actually use your VA Home Loan more than once at the same time.

I really don't know how to interact with realtors and lenders to properly use my VA Home Loan so that I am not taken advantage of.

My response: Read this book thoroughly.

**Words in BOLD are defined in the glossary (Appendix IV) **

CHAPTER ONE

Overview

In the course of 20 years serving on active duty (from 1993-2013) in the United States Navy, I have been through a lot of training. To name a few, I have been taught how to fight shipboard fires, stop progressive flooding, shipboard maintenance, combat life-saving exercises, navigation at sea using stars, and multiple other useful skills for naval services. With all the training the military has given me over the years, not once have I been taught how to properly use my *Veterans Affairs* (VA) Home Loan benefits. This book will focus on using your *VA Home Loan benefits*, and all aspects of the home buying process. I will break this process down to keep it simple *(K.I.S.S.)*, so that the most newly enlisted E1 (boot camp) in the military can easily understand and use this guide. Many times the *real estate agent* and *loan officer* often use descriptions that the everyday Sailors, Marines, Soldiers, or Airmen may not understand because they obviously do not work in the real estate field. For example, if someone in the military tries to converse to a civilian in the same manner that we talk on the ship or battle field everyday it would sound like a foreign language to them. We are going to cut through the talk that makes little sense to non-real estate professionals. Also, we are going to answer questions that some people may be too nervous to ask or may not even know how to ask when purchasing a home. Furthermore, I will also instruct you on how to use your VA Home Loan Benefits to purchase *income property* to produce a monthly profit for yourself and possibly having your mortgage paid for by tenants resulting in leaving you rent- and mortgage-free. That is if you are interested in making money, but be aware this is not a get-rich-quick type of book.

QUALIFICATIONS

Back in 2005, I decided that I was tired of renting and wanted to purchase a home for my family. I only had one problem; I had no idea how to even get started. So I did what anyone would do in my situation, I asked everyone that has already bought a house. I asked homeowner friends, co-workers, and family members of mine and they all had the same vague answers like, "just go find a home", "just get a real estate agent" or "you just got to jump right in there and get started". The way my mind works is that I require details and/or a step-by-step procedure when trying to accomplish a task I have never completed before, but I was not getting these answers from the people I knew.

Then I happened to read somewhere that *Long & Foster* were offering real estate classes close to my duty station for only $99 for an eight-week course. So on Mondays, Tuesdays, and Thursdays I attended the Long and Foster real estate class from 6 p.m. until 10 p.m. after work for eight weeks and eventually passed. My only intention was to become familiar with the home-buying process so that I would not be scammed out of hundreds of thousands of dollars when purchasing my first home. But I became fascinated with the real estate business and ultimately became a Virginia State Licensed Real Estate Agent in 2006 before purchasing my first home in August of that same year.

Due to my military obligations and frequent deployments, I did not become an *active real estate agent* until I returned home from my final deployment from Basra, Iraq in 2010 with Riverine Squadron 3. While on *shore duty* (from 2010-2013), I worked part time as an active real estate agent with Long & Foster Real Estate for two and a half years. I decided not to become a full-time real estate agent once I retired from the Navy in 2013, because the experience and hands-on knowledge I obtained as a Realtor was fulfilling enough with the knowledge I desired to become an investor. I developed skills in writing contracts, showing properties, talking with clients about their real estate concerns, negotiating with other agents, and closing on contracts. The involvement of actually working as an active agent was worth the hours I had to spend sitting in a classroom preparing for quizzes and exams.

With the information and recommendations I will offer you, you will not have to become a real estate agent or sit through any long, drawn-out classes for hundreds of dollars. This instruction is specifically for the military veteran home buyer, but can also be used by any first-time home buyer to ease some of the fears and concerns of purchasing a new home. I will expose some of the strategies that shrewd agents sometimes use on their clients so that you may avoid or counter their tactics. Moreover, I will assist you on how to correctly use your loan officer to help with the purchase of your home. By the end of this book you will be knowledgeable in the home buying process, confident in your abilities to use your VA Home Loan benefits, and competent to challenge any agent or loan officer on their duties and responsibilities to you.

CHAPTER TWO

Prerequisite I —
Veterans Affairs Home Loan

What is the VA Home Loan? Basically, it is a program that guarantees lenders and banks that if a qualified veteran or service member is approved to borrow funds to purchase a home, the Department of Veterans Affairs (VA) will ensure that the loan is paid if that service member or veteran defaults (stops paying) on the loan. To further simplify matters, you, as a veteran, can purchase a home without being required to put any money down.

Compare this to a **Federal Housing Administration** (FHA) loan, which requires the borrower to make a down payment as low as 3.5 percent of the property's cost. So, for example, if you are interested in a home that costs $225,000, you would be required to have $7,875 to put towards the down payment for an FHA loan. With the VA Home Loan you are not required to put down anything.

Even though you are not required to have a down payment, you will still need money for other things. Out-of-pocket expenses will include items such as the cost of a home inspection (approximately $350 - $450). You may also need money for the closing cost (approximately 3-4 percent of purchase price) depending on the current market (**Seller's Market** or **Buyer's Market**) and the negotiating skills of your real estate agent. If you have an experienced real estate agent, he or she will negotiate for the seller to pay for the closing cost in a buyer's market. If you have a skillful loan officer and do not wish to bring any cash to closing, he or she could have the closing cost rolled in to your mortgage loan. Furthermore, you will need money for **Earnest Money Deposit (EMD)** for an **escrow account**, which is usually $500 or $1,000 (depending on the price of the home). EMD is "good faith" money stating that your intentions are to close on a particular property during the submission of your contract offer (which we will be discussing later on in further detail). So do not be misled to think that just because it says "no money down" that you will not need to bring money to the table or have decent credit to purchase your home — but the money that you might have to bring to the table will be thousands of dollars less than if you were to use a non-VA home loan.

FAST FACT ————————————————————————

Earnest Money Deposit (EMD) is 'good faith' money

WHO IS ABLE TO USE THE VA HOME LOAN?

Answer: anyone that is serving or has served in one point or another in the United States Military can use the VA Home Loan.

To be more specific, you must have met one of the following conditions: served 90 uninterrupted days on active duty during a time of war, served 181 days of active service during peacetime, or served six years of service in the National Guard or Reserves. If you are no longer on active duty, you must have had one of these three discharges; **honorable, under honorable conditions**, or a **general discharge**. If you received an **Other than Honorable** or **Bad Conduct** discharge, you must have the VA review your specific circumstances to be approved to use the VA Home Loan benefits. Lastly, if you earned a **dishonorable discharge** from the military you will not be eligible to use the VA Home Loan.

There are some misunderstandings about the VA Home Loan benefits that many service members have that must be eliminated before we move on.

Some of the misunderstandings that fuel excuses that I have heard over the years include "I am not going to buy a house here, because I plan on moving back to my hometown when I get out the military." Some service members believe if they use their VA Home Loan benefit once they can no longer use it again. This is far from the truth; under the right circumstances you can use the VA Home Loan as many times as you want, with no limitations on the amount of times that it can be reused, given that certain criteria have been met. For example, a service member is stationed in San Diego, California and decides to purchase a home using the VA Home Loan and four years later is reassigned to Norfolk, Virginia. Once the service member sells his or her home in San Diego, their benefits are then restored and they can reuse their VA Home Loan benefits again to purchase another property at their new duty station.

Let me say this again: there is no limitation on the number of times that you can reuse your VA Home Loan benefits once they have been restored by selling the property and repaying the loan in full or partial.

Another misunderstanding is that you may only use the VA Home Loan on one property at a time, which is also not true. The VA has a set maximum dollar amount that they will allow you to use to purchase a home. The maximum amount depends on your location, and your loan officer will be able to provide that information for you. For example, if you are currently using your VA Home Loan but have begun to outgrow your home and want to purchase another, you can, as long as you do not exceed the maximum amount allowed by the VA. Consider the Hampton Roads area of Virginia, where the maximum amount allowed by the VA is $458,850. So if a service member purchases a home for $200,000 and later feels as if their family is outgrowing their current property, he or she is eligible to buy a second property as long as the next property does not exceed $258,850 — equaling $458,850 combined.

Now mind you, your intentions must be to occupy the property upon purchasing, and you must also have the credit score and income to pay for both mortgages. I do not want anyone to think that you can start purchasing a bunch of different properties at once in the Hampton Roads area not exceeding $458,850, because this is not the case.

Just a quick recap so no one gets the wrong impression: you cannot go around purchasing two or more properties at once trying to be the next Donald Trump with the VA Home Loan. In the circumstance that you purchased a home using your VA Home Loan benefits and after living there for some time (no minimum amount of time required) you have out grown it and want to purchase another to live in you may as long as:

1. You *intend* to occupy the property.

2. You are in the process of selling your current home, and both properties combined (new and old) does not exceed the maximum amount allowed by the VA in your area.

3. You plan on renting out your current home and both properties combined (new and rented) does not exceed the maximum amount allowed by the VA in your area.

4. You intend to occupy the new property and you have the income and credit to pay for two mortgages as long as both properties combined do not exceed the maximum amount allowed by the VA in your area.

Also, there is no time limit on when you must use your loan. For example, if you were discharged (not dishonorable) from the service in 1955 and never used your VA Home Loan benefit, you could still use it today. Some veterans assume there is a time limit on the VA Home loan like the time limit that used to be on the GI Bill. Service members discharged before 2013 had to use their GI Bill within 15 years, but the ability to use your VA Home Loan benefit is not bound to any time limit.

CHAPTER THREE

Prerequisite II — Understanding Your Credit

You may be a veteran with an honorable discharge or still serving on active duty, but if you are abusing your credit or do not understand how credit works you could be ineligible to use your VA Home Loan benefits at this particular time. The Department of Veterans Affairs does not set the criteria for your required or minimum credit score to become eligible; that comes from the bank or mortgage lender company. Some veterans and service members will assume that since they are disapproved by one lender then they will be disapproved by all others. Each lender has its own minimum credit qualifications. For example, let's say we have two veterans, Kim and Larry. Both are using their VA Home Loan benefits to try to secure a loan to purchase a home. Kim is attempting to use the fictional company Blue Mortgages and her credit score is 620 but they disapprove her. Then Larry uses a company called Star Mortgages and his credit score is 590 but his pre-approval loan is approved. So you should shop around if one company disapproves you with a 600 or higher credit score. I'm not saying that 600 is the magic credit score that you should be approved for, but in my personal experience I haven't witnessed anyone get approved with a score lower than 600. However, that doesn't mean that all lenders do not approve veterans with credit scores lower than 600.

As a service member, you will be a target for shady and dishonest businesses that will try to take advantage of your financial stability. Many of these businesses establish themselves in close perimeter of military bases hoping to catch the eye of trusting service members. The trained eye can spot these establishments from miles away by how they advertise themselves. They will advertise themselves by stating, "E-1 and above approved," or "Bad credit? No credit? No license? NO PROBLEM," to get the attention of service men and women.

You have to understand that to them you are nothing but a guaranteed paycheck. They are not concerned about whether you have bad, good, or no credit because they know you will get paid on the 1st and 15th of every month. They also most likely have ridiculous interest rates and if you stop paying or are late once they will simply repossess their merchandise and have your commanding officer deduct their payments directly from your paychecks. I will highly recommend that you avoid these establishments at any cost. Some examples include: payday loans, rent-to-own businesses, title loans, and car dealerships outside the base named "Honest Jim's Used Cars" or some other obviously shady name.

I have witnessed a young service member go to a rent-to-own establishment and rent a new 60-inch flat screen TV for $25 a week for 24 months (after I had already recommended that he shouldn't do it). To a young, unknowing, impatient service member this may appear to be a great deal. By the time the TV is completely paid off he would have paid three times the price it would have cost if he would have just saved his money to purchase it with cash instead of using any form of financing. In this particular case, the service member ignored the small print saying, "20 percent interest" and "if you miss one payment they have the right to repossess their merchandise but you are still responsible for the payments." Well, the serviceman was out to sea longer than expected and had missed three weeks of payments due to being on a training exercise. The rent-to-own establishment repossessed his TV, so the serviceman refused to continue to make payments on a TV he could not enjoy. This particular establishment reported his delinquent payments to his commanding officer along with the contract the service member signed. His command deducted the payments from his paycheck along with the late fees. So instead of paying three times the value of the TV, this particular service member ended up paying six times the value of that TV without even having the privilege of enjoying it. While all this was going on the business had already re-rented out that same TV to another service member paying the same ridiculous price as the previous one agreed to. Now that service member has just taken a large negative hit on his credit rating.

There are three major **Consumer Report Agencies (CRA)** that will evaluate your credit risk by assigning you a particular three-digit number from as low as 300 to as high as 850.

FAST FACT

The three main credit bureaus that lenders will use are Equifax, Experian, and TransUnion.

The CRA's risk assessment of you will determine how much a particular lender will loan you to purchase a home (or whatever you are trying to purchase with credit at the time) and at what interest rate. The lower your credit score, the higher your interest rate will be, because the lender wants to **recoup** their investment on you as quickly as possible before you decide to stop making payments.

For example, let's say we have two people, Sarah and John. Both are 22 years old, and they both work at the same job earning the same salary but John lives within his means while Sarah does not. Sarah has a **credit score** of 582 and was approved to purchase a new $30,000 car but her **interest rate** is 14 percent. John, who was also approved to purchase a similar vehicle, at the same dealership at the same price using the same lender (bank), but he has a credit score of 725 and was only charged a 4 percent interest rate. "So what?" you may be thinking. "What does it matter if John's interest rate is lower than Sarah's?" Well, Sarah's monthly car payments will be more than John's, and over the course of the loan Sarah would have paid *thousands* of dollars more than John for the exact same vehicle. You have to understand that the bank that is lending John and Sarah money to purchase these vehicles realize that Sarah is more of a risk for not paying them their money back due to her lower **credit rating**. So the bank will loan

Sarah the money but charge her a higher interest rate to recoup their money quickly just in case she decides to go back on her word and stop paying, which her low credit rating is suggesting Sarah may do.

That was just an example using cars, but the same concept is used for borrowing finances to purchase properties. As stated earlier, if your credit score is really low, you may not be eligible to use your VA Home Loan until it has risen. In my experience as a realtor I have not personally known anyone to get approved with any score lower than a 600, but every situation is different so please verify with a certified loan officer before you count yourself out.

CREDIT RATINGS			
SCORE RANGE	TITLE	DEFINITION	CONSIDERATION
800 or greater	Exceptional	Top 20 percent of consumers	Expressing to the banks and lenders that you are not a credit risk. Going to likely pay the lowest interest rates.
740-799	Very Good	Top 40 percent of consumers	Low risk to lenders
670-739	Average	Average consumer	Considered in good standards with lenders
580-669	Fair	Lowest 40 percent of consumers	Considered to be a fair score by lenders
580 or lower	Poor	Lowest 20 percent of consumers	Lenders know that you are a risky borrower. If a lender decides to allow you to borrow finances with a poor rating, you will be paying the highest interest rates available.

This information is for you to understand where you stand in the eyes of lenders and banks when they are reviewing your credit scores. You are allowed to order a free credit report on yourself once a year from each of the three main **Credit Rating Agencies (CRAs) (Equifax, Experian, and TransUnion).** I highly recommend that you order your free credit report once every year no matter what your current rating may be. You have to realize that ultimately it is your responsibility to ensure that all the information on your reports is correct. These CRAs are not perfect by any means and sometimes make mistakes or have security breaches/hacks like Equifax had in May-July 2017. The information on your report could be outdated, fraudulent, or just an honest typo. You would want to ensure that there is nothing on your report that is still being counted against you that have already paid off. Also, in this day and age, it is very easy for scammers and identity thieves to get a hold of your personal information to open up accounts in your name without your knowledge or approval. Or there could just be wrong information that made it to your credit report by mistake by someone having the same name and birthday as you. I highly recommend that you purchase the book *Credit Secrets* because it provides a step-by-step procedure for you to remove discrepancies from your credit report. Once you order your credit reports from each of the three CRAs, if you discover discrepancies on your report there will be directions on the report to inform you of the proper steps to take to correct the issues. If you need to dispute anything on your credit report, here are the addresses for the three CRAs:

Equifax
P.O. Box 7404256
Atlanta, GA 30374-0256

Experian Dispute Department
P.O. Box 9701
Allen, TX 75013

TransUnion Consumer Solutions
P.O. Box 2000
Chester, PA 19022-2000.

Credit cards can be a very useful tool to improve your credit — or they can be a nightmare and the cause of your low credit score. Ideally, you do not want to use any more than 30 percent of your available credit offered to you at any given time.

Let's say you have three credit cards: one is maxed out at $1,000, another is maxed out at $500, and the last one is completely paid off with $3,000 available credit on it. So, in an attempt to get out of debt, you cancel the card that is completely paid off. In reality, you have just damaged your own credit score. Let's examine how: you had a total of $4,500 in available credit offered to you ($1000 + $500 + $3,000 = $4,500) but were only using $1,500, or 33 percent of your available credit. By canceling the card that had $3,000 available, you went from only using 33 percent to using 100 percent of the credit available to you. By doing this, your credit score will drop drastically, so do not assume by cancelling your existing credit cards is the way to repair your credit. Also, I am not saying you shouldn't use credit cards at all because they are very useful but sometimes people tend to use them wrong and I was one of the many people that used them incorrectly in the past.

CASE STUDY

I possessed a credit card with a $24,500 credit limit. At this particular time, I had already used $16,320.21 on various items that I probably could have done without. My minimum monthly payments were $327 and I had wrongly calculated that the card would be paid off in little over four years if I continue to pay the minimum payments every month on time as long as I didn't put any more charges on it. That was not true because I had forgotten to account for the interest. I was paying 9 percent interest on the card charges and 11.99 percent interest on any cash advances I took out of any ATMs. So, out of my $327 monthly payment, $133.98 of that was only going towards the interest. In just one year I paid $1,522.85 only to the interest. So in reality, I was only paying $193.02 to the amount that I owed for the credit I actually used, and everything else was going straight into the bank's pocket through the vehicle called "interest". Now, assuming that I continued to pay only the minimum monthly payments, it would have taken me 27 years to pay this card completely off. In the end I would have paid in total $28,018 on a card that I only used $16,320.21. So I would have given away $11,697.79 of my money to this credit card company by only making the minimum payments every month.

The point of this example is to show you: Do not use your credit cards to make any purchase that cannot be paid off in two months and never pay only your minimum monthly payments. You have to understand that the credit card industry is a business and, like any business, they want to make money. They are not approving you to use hundreds or thousands of dollars of credit on their cards out the kindness of their hearts. Credit card companies are anticipating that you max out your cards and only make the minimum monthly payments. In my situation, the fine print read that if I missed a payment I would get charged a $20 late fee. Furthermore, in smaller print, it also said that, along with a $20 late fee, my interest rate could go from 9 percent to 18 percent (doubled). I eventually paid this card off (by making triple payments every month) over some time and I swore to never use a credit card again. But after rethinking the credit card situation I quickly changed my mind and the approach that I took towards them. Instead of allowing the credit card companies to take advantage of me, I decided to take advantage of them instead. My particular credit card has a reward program that grants me a certain amount of points each time I use it. So here's what I do now: I use the card for everyday items such as gas, groceries, entertainment, and anything else I would normally purchase throughout the week. I make sure that I never spend over my personal weekly budget. Then I pay the card off totally every time I get paid. So you may be thinking, "What's the point in using your credit card instead of your normal bank card?" Four things are working out in my favor.

1. Since I am paying off the total amount on the card every time I get paid, I am avoiding having to pay any monthly interest because the card is paid off before any interest can accumulate. I only pay back the exact amount that I use; nothing more, nothing less.

2. Since my card has a **reward program** associated with it, I am earning points that equal up to $100 every month. So, in reality, the credit card company is paying me to use their card. They offer this to people with hopes of you spending more than you can pay back so the interest rate can accumulate, but I never let that happen anymore.

3. My credit score is steadily improving because I am using "**revolving credit**."

FAST FACT

Revolving credit is credit that is repeatedly used and paid off every month without having to reapply for credit again.

4. I am using less than 30 percent of the available credit offered to me, which is also increasing my overall credit score.

NOTE: This procedure is also a great way for young service members who have no credit to start to build their credit in a positive (upward) direction. You may use this website to search for the best credit card for you: **https://www.creditcards.com/reward**.

Many lenders will evaluate your **FICO score** to determine the amount of risk that is involved with loaning you credit instead of viewing all three credit reports from the CRAs. FICO will calculate all three of your credit scores from the CRAs and mathematically produce one single score for you ranging from 300-850. Be aware that every lender may not use the same credit report; it is totally up to them which report they want to use when evaluating your credit. Some lenders may only use FICO, some may only use Equifax, while others use Experian or TransUnion. This is why it is important for you to ensure all the information on all three reports is accurate.

FACTORS DETERMINING YOUR CREDIT SCORE	
FACTOR	PERCENTAGE
Making your payments on time	35 percent
The amount you owe to creditors	30 percent
Length of your credit history	15 percent
New credit	10 percent
Credit mix	10 percent

Making your payments on time is the single largest factor (35 percent) when determining your credit score. The second largest factor (30 percent) is the amount you owe to creditors — how much do you owe on your credit cards or to a car dealership? So if you make all payments on time and lower the amount that you owe creditors (under 30 percent owed), you will be on your way to improving your credit score because combined that is 65 percent of determining your rating score. The length of your credit history is 15 percent of the determining factor of your credit score. You may not have too much control over that, but if you are young and on your own for the first time, I highly recommend that you obtain a credit card to start building your credit history.

Reminder: Do not use your credit card to purchase items that you cannot pay off with your next paycheck. Rule of thumb: if you can't afford to make double payments on the items that you finance then you cannot afford it. For example, if you have a car payment that is $300 then you should comfortably be able to make $600 payments. If this is not the case, then you need to rethink your decision to purchase that specific vehicle. We as service members need to make better financial decisions and realize the difference between a "want" and a "need".

Ten percent of your rating is determined by the amount of new credit you have. For example, if you recently opened up 12 different credit accounts from 12 different lenders at once, you could now be considered a risky borrower to the Credit Report Agencies and cause your credit score to go down. Also, performing multiple credit checks (not including your free credit check once a year) is considered "new credit" because you are at-tempting to open up new accounts to acquire loans which is also looked at as risky behavior. Now, if you are shopping around for the best auto or mortgage loan and must go to multiple companies within a 30-day time frame, FICO will ignore these actions. FICO understands that you are rate shopping and will not hold that against you because you are trying to ob-tain the best interest rate possible.

Lastly, "credit mix" is the final 10 percent factor in determining your credit score. Credit mix is basically the view of the different types of credit you are using at any particular time.

The goal is to never have bad credit, but if you do find yourself in that sit-uation it is not the end of the world. There are ways to improve your score; believe me, I know. I went from having a 540 to a credit score over 800. If you are having any concerns about your credit that I do not address, I ad-vise you to contact Trisha Epps at 757-270-8821 or her Facebook page, Trish-FixMyCredit. *Trish Fix My Credit* is a national credit repair service that works with individuals nationwide who are struggling with low credit scores and/or derogatory credit due to late payments, job layoffs, bank-ruptcy, repossession, and more. She also offers her clients a direct one-on-one, hands-on approach in credit repair. Her job is to help you get back on track by contacting the creditors to verify and have them validate that the information they are reporting is accurate. She provides credit coaching and education on how to rebuild your credit back the right way so that you are able to purchase homes and vehicles, and live a lifestyle that you always desired.

CHAPTER FOUR

Step One — Obtaining Your
Pre-Approval Loan

Where to begin your home search? A lot of people will begin their
search for a home with contacting a real estate agent, but I would
not recommend that for several reasons. The real estate agent has no idea
about what you qualify to purchase or if your credit will even allow you to
obtain a loan at all. If you happen to contact a real estate agent first and he
or she is not experienced, the agent might decide to start showing you
property without reviewing your **credentials**. This could result in wasting
hours, days, or even weeks looking at property that you do not qualify to
purchase. I recommend that you first seek out a mortgage loan officer
(John P. Hamilton is good reference). An experienced or knowledgeable
real estate agent is going to do this before showing you property anyhow,
but that agent is going to lead you in the direction of a loan officer with
whom they have worked with in the past. There is nothing wrong with
that. However, by conducting your own search for a loan officer, you can
shop a variety of lenders to find the one that has the best possible interest
rate for you.

When you contact a loan officer, the first thing they will do before processing your pre-approval loan is verify your **Certificate of Eligibility (COE)**
and conduct a **credit check** on you. He or she will need some personal
information from you over the phone that will only take about 10-20 minutes to obtain. Some of you will be worried that conducting a credit check
will have a negative effect on your credit rating. Also, some of you might
think that you should first pay off a few things to clear up your credit prior
to contacting a loan officer. I completely understand, but you need to know

that the Credit Report Agencies realize when multiple loan officers are conducting a credit check on you it is because you are shopping for the best interest rate, so your credit is not affected significantly. Furthermore, a loan officer will be able to help you understand which **debts** you should pay off first to have the most positive affect on your credit if you happen to have a low credit score.

So I mention this to say that if you are even slightly thinking about purchasing property, do not let these worries stop you from getting started. You might be thinking, "Well that is wonderful, but I do not have the money to pay for these acts or services today." Do not worry because you will not pay for anything at this point, the loan officer only gets paid from loan volume at the end of the transaction, which is called the "**closing.**" This process is called the **pre-approval loan**. Once you pre-qualify for a loan seek out at least two other loan officers from different companies and select the company that offers you the lowest interest rate. Now once you locate a loan officer that is offering the lowest interest rate and is willing to assist you with any and all financial issues keep his/her number on speed dial because he/she will be a powerful asset to you during the home buying process in the near future.

If you need a recommendation to get started call my personal Loan Officer John P. Hamilton, at (757) 567-2992, email john.hamilton@towne mortgage.us or visit his website **www.townemortgage.us/johnHamilton.** John can give you assistance no matter where you are located at in the United States.

NOTES

NOTES

CHAPTER FIVE

Step Two — Working With Real Estate Agents/Realtors

After you have been pre-approved through a mortgage loan officer, now it is time to select a real estate agent — but first let me share a few personal experiences of my own in dealing with real estate agents. New home buyers tend to put their real estate agent on a high pedestal and assume that they are irreplaceable, even if the agents do not fit their specific needs. During the process of my last real estate purchase I worked with *six* different agents over a period of 15 months. To any of my real estate agent colleagues that may be reading this, I assure you I did not break any exclusive buyer-broker agreement contracts during this deal. Most real estate agents will not accept you as a client until you sign an **Exclusive Buyer Broker Agreement** contract. This contract basically says that you, the client, will only work with that particular agent during the time that you are searching for properties to purchase, and if you decide to work with another agent you may be legally held responsible to pay a fee to the agent that you originally signed with. This agreement is designed to protect agents from dishonest clients that intentionally misuse realtors to view properties that they have no intention of purchasing. You have to understand that as a buyer's agent, your realtor only collects his or her fee (**commission**) at the time of closing from the seller's profit , which is usually 3 percent of the selling price. When I was an **active real estate agent**, it was standard to have clients sign an exclusive buyer's agreement contract for six months. Now the problem some new home buyers get into is that after signing this agreement with their agent, they sometimes wish they would have not signed for such an excessive amount of time. I have always felt that if I had clients that wanted out of this agreement due to our personalities clashing or whatever, I would not force them to remain in the contract, and would end it with no hard feelings. Not all agents feel this way though, and some will make their clients stay in a contract until they find a property or the time has run out.

To avoid being held hostage in an exclusive buyer's broker agreement contract with an agent that does not meet your requirements, don't ever sign these contracts for an excessive amount of time. The detail some agents "forget" to mention to their prospective clients is that these agreements can be made for any length of time. For example, you can make your exclusive buyer's broker agreement contract for three years, three months, three days, or three hours – *any length of time.* Do not try to be one of these buyers that go out and sign six different contracts with six different agents at once because this will eventually get you in legal trouble that you do not need. My recommendation is that when you are starting out, only sign this agreement for two or three weeks. Once this time has run out, if you and your agent are working well together, sign a new contract for a month, but never sign more than a month at a time. This will give you the option to move on or stay with your agent without getting into legal problems.

 Like I mentioned earlier, I had six different agents before closing on a single property during my last real estate transaction. I'm not discussing this to offend real estate agents but to make you (the veteran home buyer) understand that there are plenty of agents to choose from and if your current agent is not meeting your expectations, move on legally to the next. It was not that the five agents I had before closing were bad, but at that particular time they were not good for my situation. Too many of my friends and associates complain to me about their current agent and wish they could get out of their contracts and this is why I'm going into detail to prevent that from happening to you.

With the first real estate agent I had, I signed an exclusive buyer's broker agreement for one day before looking at properties. During the very first (and only) day that we went out to view properties I found exactly what I was looking for, which is unusual, because in my experience it usually takes a few times out before locating a prospective property. After viewing properties that day I stated to him that I wanted to put a contract on the first property (waterfront) we viewed. For reasons I do not understand, my agent waited a week and half to send me the contract to sign, which, in my opinion, is way too long. Once I received the contract via email, I signed it electronically and returned it to him as soon as possible that same day. I'm not sure what day he submitted my contract to the seller's agent, but my agent contacted me a week later to say, "Someone else already has an offer on the property." I knew at that moment that this agent was not going to work out for me because he is too laid back for my driven personality and lacks motivation in my professional opinion. I need my real estate agent to move when I need them to move, not when they want to move. As my agent, *they* work for *me*; I do not work for them, and I advise you to have a similar attitude. I simply notified him that I would not be requiring his assistance any longer and that I would not be resigning an exclusive broker buyer's agreement with him.

The second agent I had never spoke with me about signing an exclusive broker buyer's agreement contract. I'm not sure why, but if she wasn't worried about it then neither was I. Even though we never signed the exclusive broker buyer's agreement, I used her exclusively as my agent during this time. She was highly motivated, and had a large **clientele,** but the particular properties I was looking for were no longer available. We viewed over 30 properties in four months, but I did not see anything that interested me. Like I mentioned earlier, she had a lot of clients and I assume it was not profitable for her to continue to show me properties. She could be attending to clients that were not as selective as me, so she pawned me off to a lesser agent that works in her office. I fully understood and was willing to work with this agent she passed me on to, whom we will call my "third agent."

The third agent I worked with was motivated, but I could tell she was not very experienced or she had more clients than she could handle. Agent number three and I went out to view a few properties on three different occasions and all three times she was 20-45 minutes late to the viewing. After that third time, I knew she and I would not work well together because my time is more valuable to me than having her as my agent is. Just as the agent who pawned me off to her, agent number three never asked me to sign an exclusive broker's buyer's agreement, so I simply notified her that I no longer needed her assistance.

The next agent I worked with we will call "agent number four," and she is a close friend of mine that I consider family. Like the previous two agents, agent number four and I never signed an exclusive broker's buyer's agreement, but I exclusively only used her as my agent. At the time I thought to myself, "why not give a friend/family some business in real estate?" Agent number four has a regular day time job and only worked as an agent in her spare time, but nevertheless she was highly motivated. We searched for properties for almost six months together and I was starting to feel bad because I did not see anything I was interested in. Then I was starting to feel as if I was being too selective but remembered that when you are about to make a purchase over $100,000 it is wise to remain very selective. Another reason I was beginning to feel bad is because I knew she was driving over 45 minutes in one direction from her home to the areas that I specifically wanted to buy in and I could tell that this constant driving was putting an unnecessary strain on her. One particular time at the end of our partnership we had scheduled to go out and view properties just as we had done numerous times before. This time she wanted to cancel. She told me that she and her family had just recently returned from out of town and she was too tired to go view properties this weekend. Knowing her situation and fully understanding, I agreed to wait until the following weekend to view properties.

The following weekend came and we went out to view properties and on our very first stop I told her, "This is exactly what I am looking for." I also told her there was no need to continue looking at the other properties we had lined up because this was it. I wanted to write a contract and submit an offer immediately. She called the seller's agent to notify him or her we were going to submit an offer on the property and the agent said there was no need to. The seller's agent notified my friend that the property was no longer available because an offer had been submitted four days ago — three days after the date we had originally scheduled to view the property. So if we had viewed the property as originally scheduled I would already have had an offer on the home. I was heartbroken because I had already started to make plans for the property as we viewed it, but I did not blame my friend, agent number four. I blamed myself because if I was not more concerned with my friend's well-being then I could have had that property. On the other hand, if I wasn't more concerned with my friend's well-being then I would not be a very good friend. I say this to advise you to be very cautious when hiring friends or family members as your real estate agent because you may have to put their well-being before your real estate needs, resulting in your relationship suffering because of it. After this incident I felt it would be beneficial to us if we did not work together any longer to maintain our friendship.

The fifth agent I worked with was very experienced and worked as an agent full time. She did not require me to sign an exclusive broker's buyer's agreement until we found a property that I wanted to write a contract on. After about the third time out viewing homes with her, I found a property that I wanted to write a contract on. This property was not perfect but it met the requirements that I needed. The only issue with the property was that it was a **short sale**. Some real estate agents fear short sales because the process could become complicated, but not "agent number five," because she was well experienced on the subject. New home buyers assume a short sale means that the time purchasing the home will be short, but that is far from the truth. Just so you understand, a short sale means that the owners/sellers are attempting to sell the property for less (or short) than what is owed to the bank, hence receiving the name "short sale." This is usually done to prevent the property from going into foreclosure. Short sales became more frequent after the real estate industry collapsed in 2008.

The particular property I wanted to purchase was on the market for $135,000. I submitted an offer for $120,000 and the owners accepted my offer. Since this property was a short sale we also had to get the acceptance of the bank that loaned the owners the money for the property. Now be aware that waiting to hear back from the bank could take as long as four months (or longer), — makes you think this should be called a "long sale" instead. Even though I submitted an offer on the property, the contract would not be binding or valid until we had the bank's agreement. While we waited to hear back from the bank I asked my agent if we could continue to search for other properties that may be better suited for me, and she agreed. However, during the time we waited to hear back from the bank, my agent never took me out to view other properties as she said she would. When I would ask to view certain properties her responses were always the same, "That looks like a bad neighborhood," or "That house doesn't look like much," or "I'm busy this week, let's go another time," and so on. I understood what she was thinking, "We already have an offer in and I'm not going to spend unnecessary time showing you properties when I can be with other clients who do not have contracts already written." So I had to look out for myself and since our exclusive brokers buyer's agreement was only for that particular property, I searched for another agent to show me available homes until the bank responded.

I contacted "agent number six," who was a fairly new licensed agent, to show me properties; even though she was inexperienced in the real estate business she was highly motivated to show me homes. Due to the fact that I was knowledgeable in the real estate purchasing process I would gladly work with an inexperienced but motivated agent than an experienced and uninspired agent any day. This agent required that I sign an exclusive broker's buyer's agreement before showing me properties, so I signed for only 30 days. My sixth agent was eager to show me properties and, after about three weeks of viewing properties, she notified me that she had found the property I was looking for. I was not convinced with the pictures she sent me via email, but when we went to look at the property in person I realized that it was perfect. This property was in a better neighborhood, and was larger and cheaper than the short-sale property for which I had submitted an offer.

Before submitting an offer on this property, I notified my previous agent and simply stated, "I no longer wanted to purchase the short sale due to personal reasons," and she cancelled the contract and my earnest money of $500 was returned to me. I was not obligated to purchase the short sale because the bank had not yet responded. I then submitted an offer on the property agent number six found for me, and we closed on the property about 30 days later for only $110,000 dollars (originally priced/listed for

$140,000). During that process I changed agents six different times but always maintained the same loan officer, John P. Hamilton, to calculate the mortgages on each property before viewing, and I'll explain why in the next chapter. The purpose of me detailing my last real estate purchase is to show you that you do not have to settle with your current real estate agent if they are not working out for you.

NOTES

NOTES

CHAPTER SIX

Step Three — Searching for Property

In this chapter about property search, I am not going to try to recommend the type of home you should purchase or how big your yard should be, but I am going to try to assist you with avoiding some common mistakes home buyers make. I am also going to explain what to expect from your Realtor and loan officer while searching for properties.

Now that you have contacted a loan officer and have been pre-approved for a home loan, it is time to search for properties. I strongly recommend that you contact a Realtor in your area with the assistance of Google. There is no way to tell which **Realtor** will be best suited for you until you actually start working with them, but I will recommend a few highly-knowledge-able Realtors that I personally know in a few areas around the country in Appendix IV of this book.

As stated in chapter 5, initially sign an exclusive broker's buyer's agreement for only a few weeks at a time just in case you have to switch Realtors. Some new home buyers may say, "Why do I need a Realtor?" In some states it is not required to have a real estate agent to purchase or sell properties. Some sellers will try to sell their property without the use of an agent to avoid having to pay their agent's fee of 6 percent of the sale, which is standard in most areas. I can understand why some sellers would not wish to have an agent represent them for the sale of their home even though I would also highly not recommend that for multiple reasons. But anyway, there is no reason for a buyer not to want the assistance of a Realtor. For one, your agent gets their commission from the seller's portion of the sale of the property, not from you. Another reason is because Realtors can access the most recent and accurate data on properties for sale in your area. Some buyers will assume that real estate apps downloaded on their phones are just as good as having a Realtor look for properties for them. While I was an active real estate agent, I had some clients try to use these real estate apps to assist me with their search, but much of the information on there were not correct or outdated. Furthermore, if you try to use these apps and find a property that you want to buy, the next step would be to contact the agent associated with the property. By contacting the seller's agent from a real estate app without having a Realtor representative of your own, an inexperienced buyer could find him or herself in a **dual agency**. Dual agency means that the same agent represents both the seller and the buyer in the same transaction. In my opinion, it is almost impossible for one agent to be devoted to both their clients (the buyer and seller) without entering into a conflict of interest.

For example, if the agent's buyer client wants the lowest price possible and her seller client wants the highest price possible, whom does the agent help the most? Whom will her loyalty be to? In my profession opinion, her loyalty will be with her seller client (not the buyer) because the higher the sale of the house, the higher the Realtor's commission (fee) will be. This is why dual agency is not permitted in some states. In states like Virginia that do allow dual agency, it is not a position a new home buyer wants to be in. I know it sounds like dual agency may be a lot for a single agent to handle, so why would one agent take on both responsibilities? Because normally the seller is going to pay his agent 6 percent of the selling price of his property. The seller's agent will agree to pay the buyer's agent half of that (3 percent), but in dual agency one agent will keep the entire 6 percent for himself. So now you understand that dual agency could be very profitable for a Realtor in that situation but could not be in your best interest. Furthermore, another reason you need to seek out a real estate agent is because only a licensed Realtor can access the **Multiple Listing Service (MLS)** (see Appendix III), which is where the most accurate real estate information is located.

Once you locate a Realtor to your liking, he is going to ask you if you have been pre-approved to obtain a home loan. At this time you will put him in contact with your loan officer. Once the Realtor has verified that your pre-approved loan is acceptable, he will most likely want you to sign an exclusive broker's buyer's agreement contract. Now your agent will ask you for the type of home you are specifically looking for in details such as: price range, area, square footage, number of rooms, number of bathrooms, garage, etc. The more thorough you are in your descriptions, the better the agent can conduct the search. Your agent will input this information in to the MLS search engine and a list of prospective available properties will filter through to their computer. Most agents will send you this list of homes via email with pictures and comments for you to select the home you would like to view. Some agents will also setup an automatic email that will send you properties that meet your specifications once they appear in the MLS. Technically advanced agents will have their own personal website that allows their clients to access the MLS to conduct their own searches, which I personally prefer.

Now let's assume that you have chosen five properties to view out of the 20 that your agent sent to you, and you are ready to view properties. The mistake buyers make before actually viewing properties is that they do not communicate with their loan officer first. Why should you talk with the loan officer first? He is only there to process my loan, right? *Wrong.* When buyers do not consult with their loan officer they could be under the wrong assumption of what their monthly mortgage will be for each property. Not consulting with your loan officer first could result in a waste of time or you spending more money than expected every month for your mortgage.

Scenario 1: Robert is pre-approved for a loan of $300,000 but does not want to spend more than $1,500 a month on a mortgage to fit into his personal budget. After searching for properties with his Realtor, he finds a home he wishes to purchase for $275,000. His Realtor promises that his mortgage will not be more than $1,500. But, after closing on the property, Robert discovers that his monthly mortgage is $1,903 a month, which exceeds the amount he wanted to spend on a mortgage.

Like Robert, most new buyers will simply ask their Realtor for advice on what their future mortgage would be on a prospective property, because the Realtor is supposed to be the real estate subject matter expert. While in most cases that is true, your Realtor *is* the expert on all matters pertaining to real estate, but that does not make them the financial expert too. You have to understand that real estate and the finances to secure that real estate are two separate entities.

For example, you would not call a plumber to your house to work on electrical issues, or vice versa. But unlike a plumber being called to perform work he is not qualified to do, some agents will try to answer your financial question instead of saying to you, "You need to ask your loan officer." In this day and age any Realtor can simply download a mortgage calculator app on to their phone or portable devices, but this does not make him an expert in the mortgage loan business. These mortgage calculators will only give them an estimate, but your loan officer will be able to give you an accurate calculation. So my recommendation is to ask the experts the questions you have on that specific subject. You would not ask your loan officer to negotiate an offer on a property, so don't ask your Realtor about what your monthly mortgage payments will be. Once you and your Realtor locate properties worth viewing on the MLS, send the MLS information sheets to your loan officer for review. Then your loan officer can calculate all the necessary finances that will produce your mortgage. Each property will be different due to taxes and other items that your loan officer will identify due to his expertise on the subject. You must understand that this is the loan officer's job, not the Realtor's, and if for whatever reasons your loan officer cannot or will not perform this task for you in a timely manner then it is time to find a new loan officer (or call John P Hamilton at 757-567-2992) as soon as possible. It does not make sense to spend time on viewing properties that you will turn down because the monthly mortgage will be too high for your personal budget. Or even worse, you do not want to find out at closing that your mortgage is going to be $200 - $300 more than you expected — because if you are at the closing, it is too late to do anything about it.

Now let's assume you communicate to your Realtor that, although you are qualified up to $300,000, you do not want to purchase any property over $225,000. This is common. Do not be alarmed or frustrated with your Realtor if she is sending you properties that are listed for more than $225,000. Experienced agents will do this because they understand that motivated sellers could accept offers submitted for $30,000 less than the listed price.

For example, I submitted an offer of $120,000 on a property that was listed for $135,000, and the owners accepted it the first time. In another personal example, I submitted an offer of $120,000 on a property that was listed for $140,000 and the owner accepted. After conducting the home inspection on that property, I decided it was not worth my time so they reduced the price on the property to $110,000 ($30,000 less than the original price) and we closed on that deal 30 days later.

Now, if you have an inexperienced agent, he may send you properties that do not exceed your personal limits. In this case, communicate to your agent that you want to be sent properties up to $30,000 higher than your minimum requirement to possibly catch the eye of motivated (desperate) sellers in your area who might accept lower offers.

NOTES

NOTES

CHAPTER SEVEN

Step Four — Submitting a Contract

Now that you have located a property that you wish to purchase, it is time to submit a contract offer. When writing the contract, your Realtor should be explaining every sheet to you in detail. You will be required to write a check to your agent's reality company for **earnest money**. There is no set amount required for earnest money, but in my experience I've never seen anything less than $500, and nothing more than $1,000 in Virginia, but you need to consult with your Realtor for specifics. Earnest money is not a down payment; it is what we call "good faith" money. In simpler terms, you are expressing to the sellers that you have the intention with going through with this deal, and the more earnest money you submit the more seriously the sellers will take you. The earnest money will be deposited into an escrow account until closing and then the money will go towards your closing cost. If the sellers pay for your closing cost then you will receive this money back to you in the form of a check. But if, for whatever reason, you deliberately break this contract your earnest money will not be returned to you.

While the Realtor is writing your contract it is very important that you are thorough about expressing your desires. For example, do you want the existing appliances (washer, dryer, dishwasher, refrigerator, etc.) to transfer to you with the property? Or do you want the seller to purchase new appliances for you? Do you want a new fence built? Do you want new carpet or maybe hardwood floors, or maybe you want the kitchen repainted to a hot pink color? If you do not ask, the answer will be "no" 100 percent of the time. My point is for you not to leave out any details. Remember, if it is not written in the contract, then you will never know if the seller would agree to the terms. Furthermore, I would recommend that you have your Realtor state in your contract "seller to pay 4 percent of the purchase price or closing costs, whichever is greater to be used at buyer's discretion as lender allows." By using that exact phrase and terminology, your Realtor has improved your possible financial status.

> **Scenario I:** Let's say your closing cost is $5,000, but 4 percent of the purchase price is only $4,500 – you have your closing cost paid by the seller.

> **Scenario II:** Now let's say that the closing cost is only $4,000, but 4 percent of the purchase price is $6,000. Then, after paying for your closing cost, you will have $2,000 to use at your discretion within the lender's guidelines.

In a buyer's market, or when the seller is highly motivated or desperate to sell, it is common for the seller to pay for all closing costs. Like I mentioned earlier, you will never know unless it is stated in the contract. Contracts will differ from state to state, but your Realtor should be recommending these basic requests in to your contract. Your lender may ask you if you desire to "buy down points."

Buying down points is in reference to your **mortgage points**, which is basically your interest rate. One point is 1 percent of your interest rate. So, if your property is costing you $200,000 at 4 percent interest and you want to buy one point, then you will pay $2,000 (1 percent of $200,000) to get a new interest rate of 3 percent. If you are not planning on staying in the property for at least five years, it may not be beneficial to you to buy one or two points because your monthly payments may not decrease enough for you to recoup the money you paid to bring down your interest rate. If you are planning to stay in the property for at least 10 years, it may be worth your time.

For example, if buying back one or two points brings your monthly pay-ments down by $50, multiply $50 by the number of months you are planning to live there. If that number is greater than what you have paid for in discount points then it is a good investment, as long as you can initially afford to purchase the points. Some people will use the extra money left over from their 4 percent of the purchase price request from the seller to buy back points.

You should also be made aware of what to expect when dealing with bank-owned properties. Bank owned properties consist of **foreclosures**, short-sales, and **auction properties**. Banks will usually not include any repairs or upgrades to their properties and will say "**as-is**" in the description section of the MLS sheet (see appendix III). In my experience, the majority of them need some repairs. I'm not suggesting that you do not try to negotiate with the banks; I'm simply informing you on what to expect from them. Banks are already selling their properties for a huge discount and because of this they will not usually offer any repairs or upgrades due to the loss that they are already taking.

> *NOTE: Rule of thumb, your closing cost on a property $225,000 or greater is usually 3-4 percent of the sale of the property. Property costing $100,000 or lower is 5-6 percent of the sale of the property.*

If you wish to during this time, you could be informing your loan officer that you want to use the VA's acceptable **Energy Efficient Mortgage program**. This program allows veterans to roll up to $6,000 into their loan for energy-saving upgrades to the property. For example, you could have solar panels installed on the property that could cut your electricity expenses down to less than $10 a month in some cases.

Scenario: Bill is paying $227 a month on his electric bill but once he has the solar panels installed, his bill is reduced to $7, saving $220 monthly. Bill will save over $6,000 in two and a half years. Additionally, Bill would have made $7,200 in five years. In this particular scenario, our veteran Bill, will have gained a profit on his **return on investment (ROI)** in less than three years after purchasing the property and solar panels.

Please be aware that every situation will be different, so it is up to you and your loan officer to investigate to prove that this investment will be beneficial to you. If you are interested in the Energy Efficient Mortgage program, just have your loan officer assist you with filling out the proper documents upon submitting your contract to begin the qualification process for this program.

NOTES

NOTES

CHAPTER EIGHT

Step Five — Negotiations

There is no foolproof technique to negotiate a contract, but there are tools that you could use to turn the tide in your favor. Prior to submitting an offer on any property, have your Realtor conduct a **Comparative Market Analysis (CMA)**. Your agent is not required to conduct a CMA if you do not request it, so do not think they will do one automatically. A CMA will analyze the properties within a mile radius that are similar to the home you are interested in buying. More specifically, it is going to compare the homes sold in the area recently to suggest a reasonable price for a specific property. For example, you do not want to submit an offer of the full asking price of $225,000 on a property where similar homes in that area are being purchased for $190,000. The CMA is a very useful tool to employ during negotiations that will recommend a low, medium, and high price to offer — but many new home buyers never know of its existence.

Once you and your realtor have decided on a decent offer to submit on the property, contact your loan officer to produce your pre-approved letter of approval for the same amount that you are offering, not the amount that you are approved for. This is done to give the impression to your sellers that you are offering the full loan amount that you are approved for. For example, let's say you qualify for $300,000 but only want to offer $230,000 on a property that is listed for $250,000. Assuming you had a CMA conducted and the offer is reasonable, an experienced agent could convince an inexperienced agent to have their clients accept your offer. You will have the CMA results and your letter of pre-approval stating that you are using your maximum amount allowed, and if their clients are motivated they will not want to risk losing the sale by submitting a counter offer. Now, this is not guaranteed to always work but it is better than just relying on your Realtor's negotiating skills alone to get the best results.

Once you and your Realtor have decided on all the specifics of the contract, your agent will submit it to the seller's agent. Then one or the other will most likely occur: the seller will accept the offer or return with a counter offer. Then you will do one of the following: accept their counter offer, counter their counter offer, or pull your contract completely and walk away from the deal. Every deal is going to be unique in its own way so there are too many different scenarios to try and cover them all, but I think you get the idea.

Once the seller and buyer agree to the terms of the contract, it becomes ratified. Your agent will contact you and say, "We have a **ratified contract!**" Ratification of the contract simply means everyone who is required to accept the terms of the contract has signed off on it. And remember, as stated earlier, when dealing with bank-owned properties, do not expect much of a negotiation — but if you do not ask you will never know.

NOTES

NOTES

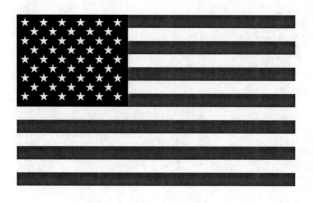

CHAPTER NINE

Step Six — The Road to Closing

N ow that you have a ratified contract, it is time to take the proper steps towards closing the deal. The majority of the actions of closing on a home will be handled behind the scenes by your agent, loan officer, and the bank's **underwriter,** but you should be aware of what is happening.

The first action your Realtor should be suggesting to you is scheduling your **home inspection**. Your agent will most likely recommend an inspector that she has worked with in the past, but you can hire whomever you wish as long as they are a licensed home inspector in your state. You will be required to pay the home inspector at the time of the inspection, usually ranging from $350-$450 up front, out of your pocket (not at closing). You have the option to skip the home inspection if you desire, but I highly recommend that you *never* skip the home inspection process. Some of you may be thinking, "Why would anyone want to skip over the home inspection process?" I have witnessed some new home buyers assume that since the property is fairly new or new construction that there is no need to perform a home inspection and can save themselves $350-450. I have also observed agents advise their clients to bypass the home inspection because a property may have been recently inspected in a previous deal that did not go through due to lack of the buyer's funding. Furthermore, during my time as an active real estate agent, I have witnessed Realtors convince their clients to skip the home inspection process, claiming that they can save them the cost of paying for the inspection because it is not required. In reality, some agents fear the home inspection portion of the home buying process because agents know that the deal could fall apart at this point.

The home inspector is going to inspect every inch of that property. You have the option to allow your agent to accompany the inspector during this process without you being present, but I do not recommend that you miss this portion. I have attended many home inspections without my clients present even though I advised them to be there, but some could not take the time off from work or had other engagements to attend. I didn't have a problem with being there with the home inspector alone, because I was going to be there anyway, but at the end of the closing, I (your Realtor) will not be the one living in the property, the buyers will be. The inspection could take a few hours, depending on the size of the home, but it will be time well spent. During the home inspection process, you (the buyer) are able to become familiar with the home because you are able to walk through the inspection with the inspector if you wish to. I would recommend that you stay side by side with the inspector, because if you close on the deal you will already be well-educated on every inch of the home in detail on the first day of officially moving in. Also, if there are any discrepancies or something that you do not like, you have the option to renegotiate the terms of your contract to include the repairs of anything that was not discovered during your initial viewing.

For example, maybe the house has old wiring that needs to be updated, or the roof needs to be repaired, or the foundation has become weakened over the years. You could request that the owner repair these items or lower the price, or both if you desire. Let's say that during the home inspection you realize that there are too many items that you don't want to deal with; you have the option to walk away from the deal totally with no penalty held against you. Some agents do not disclose this to their clients because they have the ability to walk away from the deal during the home inspection for no reason at all. This is a small loop hole that can get you out of the contract and your earnest money will be returned to you. For example, let's say that you just have a bad feeling, or you don't like the neighborhood, or you just simply had a change of heart about the whole home buying ordeal. At this point, you simply communicate in writing to your agent, "After the home inspection I no longer desire to purchase this property." Once that is expressed in writing, and with no other explanation required, you are no longer legally obligated to purchase the home. Due to this loop hole some agents may withhold this information or prefer that their clients skip the home inspection process completely.

Now, assuming that you wish to continue forward with the purchase of the property and the sellers agree to all terms renegotiated after the completion of the home inspection, let's move on. The sellers will be given a certain amount of time to complete any agreed-upon repairs or upgrades, and your agent should be keeping you updated as repairs or upgrades are completed. Now your agent should be scheduling for the property to be appraised. Even though both parties have agreed on a purchase price, in order to use the VA Home Loan, the property must appraise for no less than the loan amount. This works in the veteran buyer's favor at the end of the day. For example, let's say that the agreed sale of the property will be $225,000 but the property only appraises for $221,000. The sellers will be required to reduce the sale of the property to $221,000 or the deal is over and you just avoided buying a home that was worth $4,000 less than what you would have paid for it. On the other hand, let's assume the property's agreed price is $225,000 but it appraises for $230,000; then nothing changes, and the house will still be sold to you for $225,000, and you will purchase a home worth $5,000 more than what you paid, receiving instant **home equity**. The VA-required appraisal acceptance is a win/win situation for the veteran home buyer.

Once the home appraisal is acceptable, your loan officer will be processing your loan application for final approval. The loan officer should have been advising you since day one of this process to not take out any new loans or do anything to have a negative effect on your credit score. For example, do not open any new accounts, apply for new credit cards, or take out any new personal loans from the bank. That means hold off from buying that new car until after closing. Also, please continue to pay any current bills *on time*. This is very important, because even though you were initially pre-approved for a loan at the beginning, if you have been damaging your credit afterwards then you could become disqualified to purchase the home. Please refrain from using any credit during this whole process to ensure nothing goes wrong with your loan application. Also, do not make any deposits into your bank account that cannot be explained. The underwriter is going to be examining every deposit that was made into your bank account for the past 60 days before closing. For example, if you have a part-time job as a handyman and you are paid thousands of dollars to accomplish a large job but maybe you decided not to claim this money on your taxes (under the table). In this situation, you do not want to deposit that money into your bank account until after closing. Another example is that you begin collecting disability compensation before closing and the money required is deposited straight in to your account. This is acceptable because you will have documents to account for the extra money and where it came from. Also, be aware that if you were to accept gifts in the form of cash to assist with the purchase of your home, it is called **gift funds**. In the form of a gift fund, cash could be given to you from a friend or family member to assist with the purchase of your home. If you happen to use gift funds from an individual, the bank needs to be assured that it is not a loan and is not expected to be repaid, because that could lower your credit score and possibly make you ineligible to purchase the home. There also has to be a paper trail, meaning the lender will want to see where exactly this money came from to verify its source. For example, if your father is giving you $10,000 to help pay down your home loan, the lender will have to verify your father's bank account to see where he acquired this money and that it was transferred in to your bank account directly or in the form of a check. Also, be aware that the IRS will tax gift monies over $14,000.

Next, your agent will assist you with selecting a **title company**. The title company will conduct a title search and provide title insurance for peace of mind. This is recommended to ensure no one can try to claim your property from you in the future and to make sure there are no liens on the property. For example, let's say a previous owner left this property to a relative in a will 30 years ago but the relative never claimed the property. After you've lived in the property for five years, the past owner's relative shows up at your door to claim their inheritance. Now you have to go back and forth to court for who knows how long to try to resolve the issue. Or let's say that a previous owner forgot to pay a year's worth of taxes or had a loan taken out for repairs to the kitchen but never paid. You would be held responsible to pay these liens even though you did not live in the property at the time. The title company will ensure that there are no such issues, and if something is discovered then the seller will be required to resolve the issue before closing.

The seller should be responsible for ordering and paying for the mold and termite inspection. By this time you should have a solid closing date, and your agent and loan officer will be working hard to ensure all required documents, inspections, and repairs are made on time to ensure that they can collect their commission. There will be a **closing company** assigned to you that will be selecting a **real estate attorney** for your closing. You will be advised on which home owner's insurance companies to select but you have the option to choose the company that is best for you. Your Realtor should also assist you with selecting a home warranty company. You will be assigned an underwriter and your loan officer will lock in your interest rate. Assuming that the property is not bank-owned, the closing should take place approximately 30-45 days after having a ratified contract.

The final action required by you before closing is the **final walk-through inspection** (see Appendix II). The day before closing, you and your Realtor will walk through the property to ensure everything is still as it was before and to make sure any agreed-upon repairs or upgrades have been completed. I highly recommend that you have a checklist of all the items that you required to be repaired from the home inspection. Also, it is valuable to have a **receptacle tester** ($5 or $6 from Wal-Mart) to ensure all electrical outlets are in working condition. You will not have a licensed home inspector with you during this time, only you and your Realtor, so you want to be as thorough as possible. That's why I have included a final walk-through checklist in this book for you to use. Make sure that your Realtor does not try to schedule the final walk-through inspection the day of closing, because if there are any discrepancies it could hold up the closing process.

Now, assuming everything is to your satisfaction and there are no discrepancies in your loan process, it is time to close. Your loan officer will let you know the location, date, and time that closing will occur. He will also inform you of the amount of cash to bring with you, traditionally in the form of a **cashier's check** (recently banks are requiring that the money is wired straight into their accounts, but your loan officer will let you know the specifics). Also, it is possible for you to inform your loan officer that you do not wish to bring any cash to closing and your loan officer could roll the closing cost in to your loan. Just a rule of thumb (estimate), every $10,000 added to your loan will equal about an extra $50 added to your monthly mortgage payment. The closing cost consists of all the fees that were obtained to bring this deal together to include: lawyer fees, taxes, title company fee, loan application fee, appraisal, and the **Veterans Affairs (VA) funding fee**. The VA funding fee is a fee that the department of veterans' affairs charges to be able to self-sustain the VA Home Loan Program. Basically, this money allows the VA to be independent from borrowing money from outside sources and ensures future military home buyers are able to also use the VA Home Loan benefits. If you are using your VA home loan benefits for the first time, the funding fee will be 2.15 percent of the home's purchase price. Any time you use the VA home loan after that, the funding fee is 3.3 percent. Most veterans have their funding fees rolled in to their loan, but you can decide to pay it in full at closing if you desire. Veterans with a disability rating of 10 percent or higher are exempt from paying a VA funding fee. If you are eligible to be exempt from being charged a funding fee, you must verify your claim with your certificate of eligibility to your loan officer before closing. So if you have a service-related disability rating of 10 percent or higher, it will be your responsibility to get this information to your loan officer, because sometimes they might not ask you. Furthermore, if you have filed for disability before or while searching for a home and have not received a rating before closing, please do not worry. As we all know, it sometimes takes the VA several months to grant you a disability rating. If you are in this situation while closing on a house the VA funding fee will be applied to your loan, but if you receive a rating of 10 percent or higher, the funding fees will be returned to you by paying down your loan. Do not expect to receive a check returned to you unless you paid your funding fees with cash at closing, which most veterans do not. To retrieve your Certificates of Eligibility (COE) go to **www.ebenefits.va.gov**.

Like I stated earlier, it is possible to have the seller pay the closing cost — but that would have been identified during the negotiation phase of the process. Many new home buyers will confuse the closing cost with the down payment; no, they are not the same thing but they are two different entities. So let's assume you were not using the VA Home Loan benefits to purchase a home, you would be required to have your closing cost and down payment at the time of closing. As a veteran using the VA Home Loan, you are not required to put any money down towards the purchase of your home, but you may need money for the closing cost. The closing cost total depends on the property you are purchasing, but for a quick estimate the closing cost is usually about 3-4 percent of the purchase price for homes priced above $200,000 and 5 percent for properties $100,000 or less.

For example, if your new home is going to cost $200,000, just multiply .04 by 200,000 and your estimated closing cost is around $8,000. If the property is $100,000, just multiply 100,000 by .05 and your estimated closing cost is $5,000.

Just be aware that this is just a rough estimate and your loan officer will be informing you of the exact cost of closing. However, in a buyer's market, a good realtor will negotiate that the sellers pay for some or all of this. And remember, if the sellers only pay a portion of your closing cost, you have the option to have the remaining cost rolled into your loan, resulting in you bringing no cash to closing.

NOTES

NOTES

CHAPTER TEN

Assets & Liabilities

You also need to understand the difference between "**assets**" and "**liabilities**". Liabilities are purchases that take money out of your pockets with no intention of returning the money back to you. Also, liabilities depreciate in value over the time that you possess them. One of the biggest liability purchases that I witnessed service members make are their vehicles. Am I saying services members should not purchase vehicles? Of course not, but we should be more cautious when making liability purchases.

For example: back in 2013 I knew a E-3 who was just promoted to the next highest rank (E-4) but would not get paid for E-4 until after the first six months. So, the day after getting his promotion he went out and purchased a brand new 2013 Jeep Wrangler for $45,000. The dealership gave him $5,000 credit for his 2007 Nissan Altima trade in, giving him a balance of $40,000 being financed over 60 months. By the time he pays off the Jeep in 2018, it is only worth $19,000 in excellent condition. So, in the course of five years this particular service member gave away $25,000 ($5,000 a year) of his money. Meanwhile the used 2008 Jeep Wrangler that he could have easily purchased with 50,000 miles drives the same, with similar features, and was only $15,000. This is a called a liability because over time his purchase depreciated throughout the course of the loan.

Assets are purchases that are made that increase in value over time, or something that steadily provides you with cash. Acquiring income property is one of the most lucrative investment asset purchases you can make. Johnson could have spent less than a quarter of what he paid for his brand new vehicle to purchase income property with his VA Home Loan benefits (see Chapter 11) and the property would have paid for the Jeep. Not only could the property have paid for his vehicle, but once the property value appreciates Johnson always has the option to sell it for a greater price than what he paid for it. Under normal circumstances, you will almost never have someone purchase your vehicle from you for more than what you paid for it. Like many of us, Johnson believes that the more money he makes, the more debt he has to get into; we should not think this way, but in reversal.

CHAPTER ELEVEN

Acquiring Income Property

During my time in the military, it would have been nice to have someone else pay my rent or mortgage. Well, there was the one time I lived in military housing in Mayport, Florida for a year and a half. I thought it was a good deal at the time because I didn't have to worry about paying rent or utilities, but the Navy deducted my **Basic Allowance for Housing (BAH)** from my pay to compensate for these services. But now I'm aware it was a horrible deal because the money that they deduct while living in Navy housing would have paid for a home that could have gained equity in a house that I own. Most service members who live in military housing can only stay there while on active duty, so if someone stays there until they retire from service, they have just wasted hundreds of thousands of dollars they could have had in equity in a home that they own. What if I told you that I can show you how to live rent and/or mortgage free? This can be accomplished while using your VA Home Loan benefits, and you could collect a few extra dollars in the process. I am going to share this simple process with you, and soon you'll start saving hundreds of dollars every month.

> *NOTE: We will not be discussing the home buying process in depth during this chapter again, so please refer back to the earlier chapters for the details if need be.*

Assuming you have already been through the process of getting a loan pre-approval, and obtaining a loan officer and Realtor as discussed in Chapters 4 and 5, we are going to go straight to the property search portion. To produce an income every month, you must first start by searching for **multi-dwelling properties**. Multi-dwelling properties consist of **duplexes**, **triplexes**, **quadplexes**, or apartment-style homes (more than four units). You must ensure while searching for these types of properties that *at least one unit is vacant for you to occupy*. To be able to use your VA home loan benefits on these properties or any property, you must have the INTENT of living there upon the time of purchase. Your goal is to be able to rent out the empty units, if they are not already occupied with tenants at the time of purchase, that will either equal or exceed your monthly mortgage. Once you and your realtor have located a potential multi-dwelling property, have your realtor conduct a CMA (as discussed in Chapter 8) to know a good offer to submit. Also, you will want your Realtor to conduct a rental CMA to be made aware of what you could possibly rent out the vacant units for. Sometimes there will be tenants living in some of the units already; if this is the case you still want a rental CMA conducted to ensure that the renters are paying a rent that reflects the current market's price.

For example, you do not want to find yourself in a situation where the previous owners were renting out the units at twice the amount that should be allowed. If you find out that the rent is too high and the current renters move out, you will have a difficult time renting the units out again at that same price, which would have a negative effect on the amount of income you expect to receive. Furthermore, you do not want to have renters paying hundreds of dollars less than what they should be paying, essentially giving away your rental income.

While your Realtor is conducting the property and rental CMAs, have your loan officer calculate the prospective monthly mortgages for each property. You are looking for properties, that when the total monthly rent is calculated, it is greater than your mortgage *(Formula: mortgage – rent = a positive or equal number)*. For example: you purchase a property with three units; two units are occupied with tenants and one is empty for you to occupy. Let's assume that their rent is $500 each, equaling $1,000 rental income, and your monthly mortgage to the bank is $850. You will not only have your mortgage paid, but you will also be collecting an extra $150 (1000 - 850 = 150) each month you have tenants.

CASE STUDY

Kevin, an active duty E-4 (using his VA Home Loan benefits) and his Realtor locate a duplex on the market for sale, listed for $85,000 in Chesapeake, Virginia. This particular duplex property consists of three bedrooms, one and a half bathrooms, and 1200 square feet in each unit. Each unit is a separated structure with their own front and back yards, connected only by the front porch. One unit was occupied and one unit was empty. The unit that was occupied had tenants paying $900 a month in a market that the rental CMA suggested a rental price between $900 and $1,000. After Kevin consulted with his loan officer, he informed Kevin that his monthly mortgage would be approximately $745. Kevin's realtor negotiated for him to pay the full asking price of $85,000 and the sellers paying the closing cost along with any major damages discovered upon the home inspection. After going through the home buying process, Kevin closed on this property 39 days after obtaining a ratified contract.

During Kevin's contract offer, he submitted a check for $500 for earnest money into the escrow account, and then paid $350 cash for the home inspection. So, for this particular property, Kevin had to have a total of $850, $500 of which was returned to him at closing because the sellers paid for all closing expenses.

After purchase, Kevin's tenants living in unit "A" pay him $900 a month for rent and then Kevin pays the bank $745 a month for mortgage, leaving Kevin with $150 extra every month. Some of you may be thinking that $150 is not a lot of money, but please keep in mind that this was Kevin's first home purchase and he receives $1,245 a month for his Basic Allowance for Housing. So, in reality, Kevin saves a total of $1,400 every month that would have been used for his living expenses that someone else is paying now, and he has only been in the Navy for two years. Also, now that Kevin is technically a landlord, he receives a huge tax break every year for most repairs and upgrades to the property (please consult with a licensed tax preparer for specific tax benefits). I have heard some people complain that they don't want to have to be responsible for the repairs a landlord may have to conduct. You may hire a company to manage the property if you are concerned with making repairs or collecting rent due to frequent long deployments.

After two and a half years, Kevin now an E-5 with dependents collecting $1,608 a month for Basic Allowance for Housing, wanted to move in to a larger home closer to his base in Norfolk, Virginia. At this time, Kevin has raised the rent on his property to $1,000 a month after consulting with his Realtor. Using his VA Home Loan benefits again, Kevin purchased a single-resident home with four bedrooms, two and a half bathrooms, and 2200 square feet for $174,000. As stated in Chapter 2, this is possible because Kevin lives in an area that allows for $458,850 to be used for VA Home Loans as long as his income and credit allows. He has only used $259,000 total after his new purchase. Kevin's monthly mortgage on his new home is $1,200 and his current mortgage on his duplex is still $745, making a total of $1,945 owed to the banks every month. Keep in mind that when Kevin moved in to his new home, he rented out the duplex unit where he had been living for $1,000 a month, giving Kevin a total of $2,000 of rent that he is collecting every month. That gives Kevin a positive income of $55 every month after he pays (actually his tenants pay) his two mortgages. Add that to his Basic Allowance for Housing, and Kevin saves a total of $1,663 to do with as he pleases. Every situation will be different, but who in the military could not use an extra $1,663 monthly while having someone else pay for living expenses?

Epilogue

No one truly knows or entirely understands what we have been through or are currently going through as service members and veterans. We have had to or still do risk our lives everyday but will come back home to financial hardship. There are military families that struggle to pay their rent every month not knowing that if they were to purchase a multi-dwelling property (like a duplex) using their VA Home Loan benefits, they could have their mortgage paid for by their tenants. While serving our country, we are constantly on the move with one thing or another. We are so apprehensive with our regular military responsibilities that we sometimes do not bother or forget to invest in our own financial future. Civilians may think that going to Iraq and Afghanistan or spending months at a time out at sea to fight a war is scary, which it can be, but to some of us walking into a realty office to inquire about purchasing a home could be even scarier. The difference is that we spend months preparing and training to fight wars so when it is time to deploy we are ready to face any obstacle, but we are not trained to use our VA Home Loan benefits other than having someone point us in the direction of a real estate agent -- until now.

My motivation and intention for writing this book is not to obtain clients or a following, because I am no longer an active real estate agent like many real estate authors are. My overall goal is to relieve veterans of unnecessary stress that could be caused from the home purchasing process by sharing my 12+ years of experiences engaged in the real estate industry as a VA Home Loan benefactor, then as an active real estate agent (Realtor), and now currently as an investor. It doesn't matter if you have been in the military for only six months or as long as 33 years, or even if you have been discharged 80+ years, it's never too early or too late to utilize your Veterans Affairs (VA) home ownership benefits. Think of it like this: when you are paying rent every month, you are paying for someone else's mortgage; moreover, in fact you are building wealth for others (landlords). Property ownership is the beginning to gaining financial fortune and freedom for you and your family's legacy. Now that you have this detailed guide to instruct you on all aspects of the home purchasing process, you are empowered with the knowledge to use your VA Home Loan benefit to its full potential to invest in yourself just as much (if not more) as you have already invested in our great country

Appendix I

Veterans Affairs Home Loan Buyer's Checklist

Sequence	Action	Sat	Unsat	Date Completed	Completed By	Comments
1	Obtain Certificate of Eligibility (COE)				Veteran Buyer	Contact your command's admin personnel, your local VA office, or **VA.gov** website
2	Contact Mortgage Loan Officer				Veteran Buyer	John Hamilton (757) 567-2992 **(Highly recommended)**
3	Mortgage Pre-Approval				Loan Officer	
4	Obtain Realtor				Veteran Buyer	*see Appendix IV for recommendations.
5	Property Search				Veteran & Realtor	
6	Submit Contract Offer				Realtor	
7	Negotiate Contract				Realtor	
8	Ratify Contract				Seller & Buyer	
9	Home Inspection				Inspector, Veteran, Realtor	
10	Property Appraisal				Appraiser	

SEQUENCE	ACTION	SAT	UNSAT	DATE COMPLETED	COMPLETED BY	COMMENTS
11	Process Loan Application				Loan Officer	
12	Lock Interest in Interest Rate %				Loan Officer	
13	Obtain Title Search & Insurance				Title Company	
14	Mold & Termite Inspection				Seller	
15	Obtain Home Owner's Insurance				Veteran Buyer	
16	Obtain Home Warranty				Veteran Buyer	
17	Final Closing Actions				Closing Company & Underwriter	
18	Closing Location Disclosure				Loan Officer	
19	Final Walk-Through				Veteran Buyer & Realtor	(see Index II)
20	Transfer Utilities				Buyer & Seller	
21	Close on Property				Buyer & Closing Company	
22	Move-In				Buyer	

Final Walk-Through Checklist

ENSURE THAT REQUESTED REPAIRS HAVE BEEN MADE		
Have all the repairs you requested in your sales agreement been made?	Yes	No
Do you have all warranties and/or bills for repairs made?	Yes	No

Notes:

CHECK FOR ITEMS YOU PURCHASED WITH THE HOUSE		
Drapes	Yes	No
Appliances	Yes	No
Lighting	Yes	No
Furnishings	Yes	No
Hot tub or sauna	Yes	No
Play structures	Yes	No

Remote control devices for ceiling fans, alarms, garage doors	Yes	No
Owner's manuals for appliances and home systems (air conditioning, heating, fireplace units, alarm systems, etc.)	Yes	No
Other:	Yes	No

Notes:

CHECK WINDOW AND DOORS

Do the doors open and close properly?	Yes	No
Do the windows open and close properly?	Yes	No
Do the windows latch?	Yes	No
Are any windows missing screens?	Yes	No
Are there any missing storm windows?	Yes	No
Is there condensation in double-panned windows?	Yes	No
Are there any broken windows?	Yes	No

Notes:

CHECK FOR MOLD AND WATER DAMAGE

Do the windows have signs of mold?	Yes	No
Are there signs of mold or water damage under the kitchen sink?	Yes	No
Are there signs of mold or water damage in the bathroom?	Yes	No

Are there signs of mold or water damage around the refrigerator area?	Yes	No
Are there signs of mold or water damage around the washer/dryer area?	Yes	No
Are there signs of mold or water damage around the water heater?	Yes	No

Notes: **Mold can begin growing within 48 hours and water damage can occur at any time. So, even if your physical inspector did not find signs of mold or water damage, you should look for these during the final walk-through.**

CHECK APPLIANCES AND SYSTEMS

Start the dishwasher when you come in. Can it complete its cycle?	Yes	No
Test the air conditioner. Does the thermostat work? Does the system blow cool air?	Yes	No
Test the heating system. Does it get hot?	Yes	No
Flip on overhead fans. Do they work?	Yes	No
Test the water heater. Is the water from faucets hot?	Yes	No
Does the doorbell work?	Yes	No
Does the security alarm work?	Yes	No
Does the intercom work?	Yes	No
Does the garage door open and close smoothly and quietly?	Yes	No
Does the washer work?	Yes	No
Does the dryer work?	Yes	No
Does the stove work (check all burners and oven)?	Yes	No

Does the built-in microwave oven work?	Yes	No
Does the damper in the fireplace work?	Yes	No
Does the gas come on in the gas fireplace?	Yes	No
Does the fan work in the gas fireplace?	Yes	No

Notes:

CHECK INTERIOR FLOORS, WALLS, AND CEILINGS

Are there water stains on the ceiling (especially below bathrooms)?	Yes	No
Have any walls been damaged by movers?	Yes	No
Are handrails in stairways secured?	Yes	No
Have floors been damaged by movers?	Yes	No
Have the floors been damaged by pets?	Yes	No

Notes:

CHECK FOR LEAKS AND PLUMBING PROBLEMS

Flush all toilets. Do they run, empty slowly, or leak?	Yes	No
Check all faucets. Do they leak?	Yes	No
Fill the sinks. Do they drain properly?	Yes	No
Fill the tubs. Do they drain properly?	Yes	No

Do the overflows on the tubs work?	Yes	No
Do the tub jets work? (spa tubs only)	Yes	No
Turn on all showers. Do they drain properly?	Yes	No
Check the basement. Look at the floor, walls, and any exposed plumbing. Are there signs of leaks?	Yes	No

Notes:

CHECK ELECTRIC

Turn on all lights. Do they work?	Yes	No
Check plate covers. Are they damaged or missing?	Yes	No
Check the kitchen and bathroom outlets. Are there GFCI outlets next to the sinks and other water sources?	Yes	No
Inspect the circuit breaker box. Are all the circuits labeled?	Yes	No

Notes:

CHECK EXTERIOR

Is the landscape as you expected it?	Yes	No
Turn on the sprinklers. Do they work?	Yes	No

Notes:

CHECK ATTIC AND OTHER STORAGE PLACES

Is it empty?	Yes	No
Do you see signs of pests?	Yes	No

Notes:

CHECK FOR CLEANLINESS

Is the property clean overall?	Yes	No
Is all personal property not included in the sale removed?	Yes	No
Are there signs of bug infestations?	Yes	No
Is all debris removed?	Yes	No

Notes:

Sample MLS Listing

List#1234567	*EXAMPLE* 6578 Main Street	Detached Residential

Ownership: Simple
Date Listed: 2/14/17
Date Entered: 2/14/17
Date Updated: 9/14/17
Date Off-Mrkt:
Date Expire: 2/14/18
Date Closed:
Financing:
Owner: DAVID E NELSON JR – Phone (555) 123-4567
Showing: CALL or TXT AGENT
Possession: SETTLE

$210,000 ACTIVE

Photo Code: Listing Agent
Original Price: $250,000
List Price: $210,000
Sale Price:
Selling Ofc:
Selling Agt:
Sold Terms:

Lockbox: Personal Lockbox

LO: 1234- *John P Hamilton - (757) 567-2992*
LA: 23872- Cassandra Simpson –
Ph: 757-751-0482
LA2:
LA Email: letsimpsonsellit@gmail.com

Fax: 1-866-298-0890
LA Oth Ph:
SBC: 3%

List Type: Standard Agency ER
Sub Agt: No
BBC: No
SCA: No

Addr: 6578 Main Street
Area: 22- Northwest Portsmouth
Legal: LT 87 BISHOP GREEN SEC1

City/Zip: Portsmouth, VA 23703
Subdiv: 157- BISHOPS GREEN
Neighbrhd: BISHOPS GREEN

Parcel ID: 0900000590
Zonning: RS-100
AICUZ: Crash: None/Noise: -65

# Stories: 1.0	Fireplace: 1	Appx Lot Frnt:	**High School**: Churchland
Bedrooms 4	Appx Yr Blt: 1995	Appx Lot Dpth:	**Middle**: Churchland Middle
Full Baths: 3	New Cnstr: No	Appx Dim:	**Elementary**: Churchland Academy
Half Baths: 1	Mstr Model: No	Appx Acres: 0.45	Other:
# Rooms: 8	Fence: Yes	Fence Desc: Back Fenced	
Appx Sq Ft: 2,366	Waterfront: No	View:	

	Level	
Living Room:		**Heating**: Natl Gas
Great Room:		**Cooling**: Central Air
Dining Room:		**Wtr Heater**: Gas
Kitchens:		**Water**: City/County
Family Room:		**Sewer**: City/County
Master Room:		**Efficiency**:
Utility Level:		

Foundation: Slab
Siding: Vinyl
Floors: Hardwood, Carpet
Roof: Asphalt Shingle

Appx Mtg Bal:
Mtg Pmt:
Mtg Yrs:
Mtg Int:

MCOA:
Pmt Incl:
Mtg ROL:
Mtg SOE:

Type Mtg:
Seller Cont:
Appx Taxes: $2,575
Seller Finance: None

MO POA Fee:
Condo/Coop Fee:

Agent Remarks: Short Sale pending lender approval. Lock box on side of garage door for use on back door/ Vacant txt LA and go show!

Public Remarks: BEAUTIFUL 4 BR/3.5 BA HOME BEING SOLD AS IS, MSTER BTH W/FIREPLACE, SKY LIGHTS, CATHEDRAL CEILINGS, WALK IN CLOSET FRIENDLY NEIGHBORHOOD, OPEN FLOOR PLAN, EATIN KITCHEN, ENTERTAIN ON THE EXTENDED PORCH W/HOT TUB. SECURITY SYSTEM/LIGHTS IN HOUSE, VACCCUMING SYSTEM.

Directions:
Style: Traditional
Accessibility:
Equipment: Cable TV Hookup, Ceiling Fan, Central Vac, Gar Door Opener, Hot Tub, Jetted Tub
Appliances: Dishwasher, Disposal, Dryer Hookup, Washer Hookup
Interior Feat: Cathedral Ceiling, Gas Firepl, Mstr Bdr Firepl, Skylights, Walk-In Closet, Window Treatments
Exterior Feat: Deck, Patio
Waterfront: Not Waterfront
Other Rooms: Attic, Breakfast Area, Fin. Rm Over Gar, Foyer, Mstr Bdr w/ Bath, Pantry
Parking: Garage, 2 Car, Attached
Amenities:
Pool: No Pool
Sustainability:
Green Cert:
Miscellaneous:
Agncy Apprvd: All
Contingencies:
Disclosures: Short/Comp Sale, Disclosure Statement

Condo Level:
Unit Desc: 1 Living Lvl
Assoc Mgmt:
Web Excl

MLS Sectional Breakdown

- In the upper left hand corner of the MLS there is a seven-digit number to identify that property. Each property **listed** (for sale) will be assigned a specific MLS number. When communicating with your Realtor about properties you are interested in, it may be quicker for your agent to find the property if you use the MLS numbers instead of the address. To the right of the MLS number you will find the property's plain address. Lastly, on the far right at the top of the MLS sheet you will find the property's type (residential, detached, condos, multi-family, etc.).

- In the first row directly under the MLS number to the far left you should see a picture of the property. If you are reviewing the MLS from a computer or a portable device that can access the internet you should be able to click on the picture and view all pictures associated with the property. In my personal experience as a Realtor, when there was only one picture uploaded in to the MLS that usually meant that the rest of the house was not worth taking pictures of. With that being said, if the listing is brand new the listing agent may not have had time to upload pictures for the property yet; but if it has been listed for a year and there is only one picture loaded be prepared for damages in the inside.

- In the first row to the right of the property's picture there is a brief description about the listing. This information includes the date the property was listed and the current asking price; if the property was reduced in price it will also show the original asking price. With this information you may be able to identify if the sellers are desperate to sell. For example, if you are interested in a certain property that has been listed for about 12 months or so and has been reduced in price several times, then you are most likely dealing with "motivated sellers". More than likely the sellers are desperate to sell and will accept an offer lower than what the property is listed for. Furthermore, in this section they may or may not have the owner's name and information about how your agent can set up appointments to gain access to the property for a showing.

- The information in the second row far left is mostly for your agent. This area will have the lending officer's (LO) and listing agent's (LA) contact information, email, phone number, and fax number to submit contact offers. If there is a sub-agent associated with the property, that information will be located here along with the type of listing this is. Just be aware that on your report the majority of this information may not be available to you because your Realtor may not want you to have this information, which is a good idea. Some buyer clients may feel that it is okay to contact the listing agent but that is never a good idea. Let your Realtor do his job and never contact the sellers or/and the listing agent.

- The third row beginning to the far left contains the address specifics, such as the exact area, city, zip code, sub-division, and neighborhood name. This is important for you so that you may conduct thorough research on the surrounding areas to familiarize yourself with the status of that area. Many buyers will ask their Realtor if the area the property is located in is safe. When I was a Realtor in Virginia, it was illegal for us to advise clients on the conditions of any neighborhood because it could be considered **steering**. Whether your Realtor tells you a neighborhood is good or bad, I highly advise you to conduct your own research. There are websites that will tell you the crime level in each area — or simply drive by the property late on a weekend night to see for yourself.

- The fourth row beginning to the far left is where you will locate the number of bedrooms, bathrooms, half bathrooms, and total number of common rooms inside the home. This section will also supply you with the year the property was built, the total square footage, if there is a fireplace, fence, waterfront, if this is new construction, and the approximated acres the property sits on. To the right of this section are the elementary, middle, and high schools your children will be attending if you have school age children living with you.

- The fifth row is where you will find the property's heating, cooling, water, and sewage sources, along with the foundation, siding, flooring, and roofing material.

- The sixth row is where you will locate the taxes associated with the property, which is very important to your loan officer to compute your monthly mortgage. On the far right it will disclose if there are any condo fees or MO POA (Monthly Property Owner's Association) fees, commonly known as a Home Owners Association. If there are any of these types of fees, you will want to know exactly what the fees are paying for. Usually the home association will ensure everyone keeps up their homes to maintain the neighborhood's property value. Also, in some areas it also pays for the usage of swimming pools, tennis courts, clubhouses, and other recreation areas commonly used by all residents. Furthermore, you may have to get permission from the HOA to make any upgrades to your property or you will be finned monthly until you get approval or return the property to its original state

- The seventh row is going to be the agent remarks that you may not have on your MLS report. These are remarks left by the **listing agent** for the buyer agent's use only. For example, it may say, "need 24 hours' notice to schedule a showing" or "Lockbox is on the back door, property is empty, go show now, lockbox code is 1234." Like I stated earlier, you may not have this section on your MLS and that is fine.

- The eighth row is the listing agent's remarks about the property in their own words. The listing agent gives a brief description about the property to attract buyers to the home. If you see phrases like "as-is," that usually means that the property is bank-owned, like a foreclosure or a short sale. If you see the phrase "motivated seller," that tells you that the owners are most likely willing to accept an offer lower than the current listing price.

- The very last section is filled with many miscellaneous items about the property that may interest you. This information includes equipment, appliances, parking, other rooms, and exterior and interior features.

An outstanding listing agent will ensure that their MLS listing is filled out in detail. The more information inserted on the MLS the better chance she will have buyers attracted to the listing. With that being said, you may come across some listings that are not completely filled out because the agent was in a rush or maybe they just forgot some items. If you come across an incomplete MLS just notify your Realtor and he will get any information not already supplied for you on the MLS.

Recommendations

Realtors ®:

Hampton Roads (7Cities) Surrounding Virginia Areas:
Cassandra Simpson with 1st Class Real Estate, Ph. 757-751-0482
Associated Broker/ Military Relocation Specialist
2540 Virginia Beach Blvd, VA Beach, VA 23452
letsimpsonsellit@gmail.com
www.simpsonsells757.com

Hampton Roads (7Cities) Surrounding Virginia Areas:
Claudine Ellis with Keller Williams, Cell 757-353-7979/
Office: 757-361-0106
Broker,ABR,CMP,CRS,CSP,GRI,MCSP,MIRM,RELOCATION
1100 Volvo Parkway, Chesapeake, VA 23320
dreamgirlsrealestate@gmail.com
www.dreamgirlsrealestate.com

Baltimore, Maryland and Surrounding Areas:
Charles Barnett with Permira Realty LLC, Ph. 410-522-1078/FAX:
410-522-1079
Premier Property Management Investment LLC
400 W Franklin St. Ste 400, Baltimore MD 21201
Charles.Barnett@ppmillc.com
www.ppmillc.com

Washington DC, Southern Maryland and Northern Virginia surrounding areas (DMV)
Koki & Associates, Inc.
Long & Foster Real Estate
2300 Calvert St NW
Washington, DC 20008
direct: 202-238-2888
main office: 202-483-6300
Email: koki@kokiisthekey.com
Facebook.com/Kokiisthekey

Fayetteville, NC and Fort Bragg Surrounding Areas:
Jessica Thompson
Coldwell Banker Advantage Cell; (910) 489-8194 Office; (910) 483-5353
3800 Raeford Road
Fayetteville, NC 28304
Email: jthompson@homescba.com
Website: www.talktothompson.com

Jacksonville, NC and Camp Lejeune Surrounding Areas:
Emily Rideout
Coldwell Banker Sea Coast Advantage Cell (910) 545-2076
Castro Real Estate Team Office Number (910) 353-5100
2355 Western Blvd Suite 300
Jacksonville, NC 28546
Email: rideout@gmail.com
Website: www.erideout.seacoastrealty.com

Atlanta GA and Surrounding Areas
Rod Williams, Top Producing Realtor
Solid Source Realty, Inc Cell (404) 966-2562, Fax (678) 519-2737
10900 Crabapple Rd
Roswell, GA 30075
Email: 404realestate@gmail.com
Website: www.SolidSourceRealty.com

Jacksonville Florida and Surrounding Areas
Denise Turner with Future Home Realty, Cell 904-588-5391
Realtor
12443 San Jose Blvd # 703, Jacksonville FL
www.askdeniseturner.com

Southern Florida Surrounding Areas:
Joseph "Tony" DeFalco with 93 Realty, Ph. 561-352-6759
Broker/Owner
10555 Oak Meadow Lane, Lake Worth, FL 33449
tonydefalcoagent@gmail.com

Central/San Antonio Texas and Surrounding Areas
Derrick Miller with JB Goodwin Realtors, Cell 478-357-7693
Graduate Realtor Institute, GRI
U.S. Military on the Move Expert
U.S. Army Retired
18503 Sigma Rd, Suite 100, San Antonio, TX 78258
Derrickmiller@jbgoodwin.com
www.jbgoodwin.com

San Diego California and Surrounding Areas
Gabe Mendez with The Associates Realty Group CA B.R.E #01937611,
Ph.619-876-2265
Real Estate Consultant
MendezRGabriel@gmail.com
www.GabeMendez.realtor

Mortgage Loan Officer:

John P. Hamilton 757-567-2992
Email: john.hamilton@townemortgage.us
Website: www.townemortgage.us/johnHamilton

Credit Repair Services:

Trisha Epps 757 270-8821
Facebook page: Trish Fix My Credit

Denise Turner 904-588-5391
Email: dtnfl66@gmail.com

Book:

"Credit Secrets"
https://creditsecret.org

Free Phone application

"Credit Karma" used to monitor your credit reports, check credit score anytime and review credit tips

Glossary

Active Real Estate Agent - working on behalf of a licensed real estate broker, is a licensed professional who works on behalf of the buyer and seller of real estate during a sales transaction

Appraisals - The act of estimating or judging the nature or value of something or someone

As-is - the buyer is buying an item in whatever condition it presently exists, and that the buyer is accepting the item "with all faults", whether or not immediately apparent

Assets - property owned by a person or company, regarded as having value and available to meet debts, commitments, or legacies

Associated Broker - A licensed broker whose license is held by another broker. An associate broker qualifies to be a real estate broker but still works for and is supervised by another broker

Auction Properties an **auction** is a **property** that will be sold at a public forum. Auction listings have a starting bid (or reserve) price. Banks may try to sell homes at auctions in order to avoid selling them as foreclosures.

Bad Conduct - a discharge of a person from military service for an offense less serious than one for which a dishonorable discharge is given

Basic Allowance for Housing (BAH) - is a United States military privilege given to many military members. It was previously called Basic allowance for quarters (BAQ).

Buyer's Market - A real estate market in which there are more sellers and homes for sale than buyers. The buyer has the upper hand in negotiating due to the larger amount of people selling than purchasing homes at the time.

Broker - an agent who buys or sells for a principal on a commission basis without having title to the property

Cashier's Check - a check guaranteed by a bank, drawn on the bank's own funds, and signed by a cashier. Cashier's checks are treated as guaranteed funds because the bank, rather than the purchaser, is responsible for paying the amount. They are commonly required for real estate and brokerage transactions.

Certificates Of Eligibility (COE) - a document issued by the Veterans Administration (VA) to those veterans qualified for VA guaranteed loans for homes, business, and mobile homes. A certificate of eligibility from VA is one of the most important documents required to apply for a new VA loan.

Client - A client or principal is someone who has authorized an agent to represent their interest in a matter.

Clientele - clients collectively

Closing (also referred to as completion or settlement) — the final step in executing a real estate transaction.

Closing Company - A company or firm that conducts real estate closings, also called settlements. The closing company does not represent any party to the transaction, but merely ensures that all documents are properly signed and all monies collected and disbursed according to the parties' contract.

Closing Costs - fees paid at the closing of a real estate transaction. This point in time called the closing is when the title to the property is transferred to the buyer.

Consumer Report Agencies (CRA) - any person which, for monetary fees, dues, or on a cooperative nonprofit basis, regularly engages in whole or in part in the practice of assembling or evaluating consumer credit information or other information on consumers for the purpose of furnishing consumer reports to third parties, and which uses any means or facility of interstate commerce for the purpose of preparing or furnishing consumer reports. Lenders go to the three main credit bureaus — Experian, TransUnion, and Equifax — when looking to pull and review your credit reports. There are numerous CRAs in the business besides these three agencies.

Commission - a fee paid to an agent or employee for transacting a piece of business or performing a service; especially: a percentage of the money received from a total paid to the agent responsible for the business.

Comparative Market Analysis - an examination of the prices at which similar properties in the same area recently sold. Real estate agents perform a comparative market analysis for their clients to help them determine a price to list when selling a home or a price to offer when buying a home.

Credentials - a qualification, achievement, personal quality, or aspect of a person's background, typically when used to indicate that they are suitable for something

Credit - Money that a bank or business will allow a person to use and then pay back in the future. A record of how well you have paid your bills in the past.

Credit Check - The process of evaluating an applicant's loan request or a corporation's debt issue in order to determine the likelihood that the borrower will live up to his/her obligations

Credit Score - a number assigned to a person that indicates to lenders their capacity to repay a loan. [*Very Poor 580 or lower*],[*Poor 580-669*],[*Average 670-739*],[*Good 740-799*],[*Excellent 800 or higher*]

Credit Rating - an estimate of the ability of a person or organization to fulfill their financial commitments, based on previous dealings

Debts - something, typically money, that is owed or due

Dishonorable Discharge - the dismissal of someone from the armed forces as a result of criminal or morally unacceptable actions

Dual Agency - occurs when a single real estate agent represents both the buyer and seller in a real estate transaction. A dual agent must be loyal to both the buyer and the seller.

Duplexes - a dwelling having **apartments** with separate entrances for two households. This includes two-story houses having a complete apartment on each floor and also side-by-side **apartments** on a single lot that share a common wall.

Earnest Money - money paid to confirm a contract

Earnest Money Deposit (EMD) - Earnest money is a deposit made to a seller showing the buyer›s good faith in a transaction. Often used in real estate transactions, earnest money allows the buyer additional time when seeking financing. Earnest money is typically held jointly by the seller and buyer in a trust or escrow account.

Energy Efficient Mortgage Program - a mortgage that credits a home's energy efficiency in the mortgage itself

Escrow - a legal concept in which a financial instrument or an asset is held by a third party on behalf of two other parties that are in the process of completing a transaction

Equifax - a consumer credit reporting agency in the United States, considered one of the three largest American credit agencies along with Experian and TransUnion

Exclusive Buyer's Broker Agreement - You are agreeing to work solely with the broker and, by extension, the agent you have selected. This means you should not ask a different broker to show you property nor write a purchase offer for one.

Experian - a global information services group with operations in 40 countries

Federal Housing Administration - a mortgage issued by federally qualified lenders and insured by the Federal Housing Administration (FHA).

FHA loans are designed for low- to moderate-income borrowers who are unable to make a large down payment.

FICO Score - a person's credit score calculated with software from **F**air **I**saac **CO**rporation (FICO)

Final Walk-Through Inspection - an inspection performed anywhere from a few hours to a few days before settlement. Its primary purpose is to make certain that the property is in the condition you agreed to buy — those agreed-upon repairs, if any, were made, and nothing has gone wrong with the home since you last looked at it.

Foreclosures - the action of taking possession of a mortgaged property when the mortgagor fails to keep up their mortgage payments

General Discharge - a form of administrative discharge. If a service member's performance is satisfactory but the individual failed to meet all expectations of conduct for military members, the discharge is considered a General Discharge, Under Honorable Conditions.

GI Bill - the GI Bill created a comprehensive package of benefits, including financial assistance for higher education, for veterans of U.S. military service.

Gift Funds - money or assets that one person transfers to another while receiving nothing or less than fair market value in return. Under certain circumstances, the IRS collects a tax on gifts.

Home Inspection - a non-invasive visual examination of a residential dwelling, performed for a fee, which is designed to identify observed material defects within specific components of said dwelling

Home Equity - the market value of a homeowner's unencumbered interest in their real property — that is, the difference of the home's fair market value and the outstanding balance of all liens on the property

Honorably Discharged - discharge from military service with a favorable record

Income Property - property bought or developed to earn income through renting, leasing, or price appreciation. Income property can be residential or commercial.

Intentions - a thing intended; an aim or plan

Interest Rate - the amount charged, expressed as a percentage of principal, by a lender to a borrower for the use of assets

Investor - a person or organization that puts money into financial schemes, property, etc. with the expectation of achieving a profit

K.I.S.S. - an acronym for "Keep it simple, stupid" as a design principle noted by the U.S. Navy in 1960. The KISS principle states that most systems work best if they are kept simple rather than made complicated; therefore simplicity should be a key goal in design and unnecessary complexity should be avoided.

Lenders - an organization or person that lends money

Liabilities - a thing for which someone is responsible, especially a debt or financial obligation

Liens - a right to keep possession of property belonging to another person until a debt owed by that person is paid

Listed - a real estate sale transaction in which a specified real estate agent stands to gain a commission if a property sells within a specified number of months, no matter how a buyer is found

Listing agent - a real estate agent that helps homeowners sell their home. Listing agents list client homes on the MLS and negotiate the best possible price and terms for the home seller.

Loan Officer - representative of banks, credit unions and other financial institutions that find and assist borrowers in acquiring loans

Long & Foster - the United States› largest privately owned real estate company and the largest global affiliate of Christie›s International Real Estate

Mortgage Points - also known as discount points, are fees paid directly to the lender at closing in exchange for a reduced interest rate. This is also called "buying down the rate," which can lower your monthly mortgage payments. One point costs 1 percent of your mortgage amount (or $1,000 for every $100,000).

Multi-Dwelling Properties - a classification of housing where **multiple** separate housing units for residential inhabitants are contained within one building or several buildings within one complex

Multiple Listing Service (MLS) - a **service** used by a group of real estate brokers. They band together to create an **MLS** that allows each of them to see one another's **listings** of properties for sale. **(also see Appendix III)**

Pre-approval loan - the initial step in the mortgage process. You supply a bank or lender with your overall financial picture, including your debt, income, and assets. After evaluating this information, a lender can give you an idea of the mortgage amount for which you qualify. People interested in buying a house can often approach a lender, who will check their credit history and verify their income, and then can provide assurances they would be able to get a **loan** up to a certain amount.

Prerequisite - a required prior condition. If something is required in advance of something else, like if you have to take a beginning Spanish class before signing up for Spanish II, then it's a prerequisite. Add pre meaning "before" to require and you have something that's "required before."

Quadplex - Also called fourplex. A building having four dwellings or commercial units.

Ratified Contract - acceptance or confirmation of an act or agreement that was signed (executed) by the confirming party itself

Real Estate Agent - a person who sells and rents out buildings and land for clients

Real Estate Attorneys - also often handle a closing on a purchase. This is when an individual or entity purchases a piece of **real** property from another person or entity.

Realtor – a person who works in the real estate business and is a member of the National Association of Real Estate Boards, or one of its constituent boards, and abides by its Code of Ethics.

Receptacle Tester - is a device used to verify that an AC wall outlet is wired properly. The tester itself is small device containing a power plug and several indicator lights.

Recoup - regain (something lost or expended)

Return On Investment (ROI) - measures the gain or loss generated on an investment relative to the amount of money invested

Revolving Credit - credit that is automatically renewed as debts are paid off

Reward Program - an incentive program operated by credit card companies where a percentage of the amount spent is paid back to the card holder

Seller's Market - homes will be higher priced and more attractive to the sellers in the market. Sellers have the upper hand in negotiating due to the larger amount of people purchasing than selling homes at the time.

Shore Duty - Naval service at land bases

Short Sale - a sale of real estate in which the net proceeds from selling the property will fall short of the debts secured by liens against the property. In this case, if all lien holders agree to accept less than the amount owed on the debt, a sale of the property can be accomplished.

Steering - the practice in which real estate brokers guide prospective home buyers towards or away from certain neighborhoods based on their race. Racial steering is often divided into two broad classes of conduct; Advising customers to purchase homes in particular neighborhoods on the basis of race.

Under Honorable Conditions - (OTH) An OTH is a form of administrative discharge. Generally, in order to receive VA benefits and services, the veteran's character of discharge or service must be under "other than dishonorable" conditions.

Underwriter - Mortgage underwriting in the United States is the process a lender uses to determine if the risk of offering a mortgage loan to a particular borrower under certain parameters is acceptable.

Title Company - a company involved in examining and insuring title claims for real estate purposes. The company verifies ownership of real property and determines the valid owner through a thorough examination of property records in a title search. The title company usually does an abstract of title.

TransUnion - an American company that provides credit information and information management services to approximately 45,000 businesses and approximately 500 million consumers worldwide in 33 countries. It is also the third-largest credit bureau in the United States.

Triplexes - a building divided into three self-contained residences

VA Funding Fee - a set fee applied to every purchase loan or refinance. The proceeds go directly to the VA and help cover losses on the few loans that go into default.

VA Home Loan - a mortgage loan in the United States guaranteed by the United States Department of Veterans Affairs (VA)

Veterans Affairs - Department of Veterans Affairs (VA) The second-largest cabinet department, the VA coordinates the distribution of benefits for veterans of the American armed forces and their dependents. The benefits include compensation for disabilities, the management of veterans› hospitals, and various insurance programs.

Index

About the Author

David Eugene Nelson, Jr. joined the Navy at 17 years old in 1993 as an undesignated seaman recruit (E-1) from Baltimore, Maryland. Before retiring from active duty in 2013, he had worked his way up the ranks to achieve the title of Chief Boatswain's Mate (E-7). David spends a lot of his time now investing in real estate and occasionally assisting friends as they go through the home purchasing process. He recognized that many of his friends were making the same mistakes that he himself made in the past. Understanding that there could possibly be thousands of service members and veterans making the same mistakes, David decided to write this short guide. This book is meant to be used as you go through the home purchasing process so you can mold your own blueprint to home ownership. If you'd like to contact David, please email him at denelsonjr3@gmail.com.